Heli Ryhänen

Heli Ryhänen

Unscharf
Out of the blur

SilvanaEditoriale

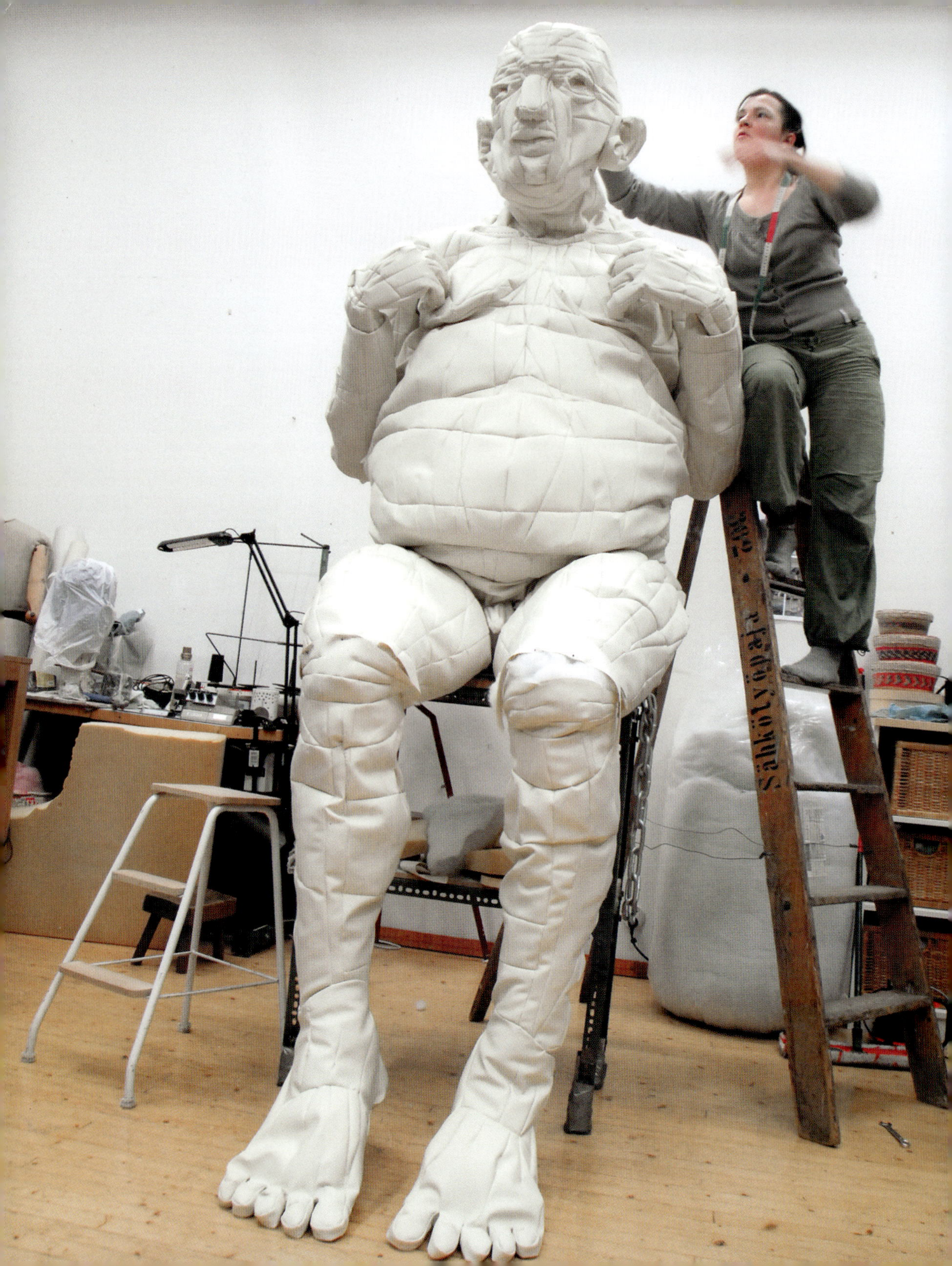
Sähkötyöpaja

Inhalt / Contents

Wir kennen den Kontur
des Fühlens nicht: nur,
was ihn formt von außen

Rainer Maria Rilke, *4. Duineser Elegie*

We don't know the contour
of feeling, only what shapes
it from outside

Rainer Maria Rilke, *Fourth Duino Elegy*, in *Duino Elegies*,
translation by David Oswald, Einsiedeln: Daimon, 1997

Die das vergangene mit dem neuen Jahrhundert verklammernde Diskussion über die Inszenierung des Körpers, über seine Fragmentarisierung, seine Formung und gentechnische Reproduktion, lässt den Betrachter der Plastiken der finnischen Bildhauerin Heli Ryhänen vielleicht vorschnell an einen feministisch-zeitkritischen Kommentar zum Körperkult denken. Schließlich versucht die Gender-Debatte nachhaltig, Männer- und Frauenbilder zu dekonstruieren, die vorher patriarchalische Strategien konstruiert haben[1]. Die Apologien einer trans- oder ahumanen Wissenschaft fordern permanent eine künstlerische Beschäftigung mit dem Körper heraus.

The debate over the ways the body is staged, its fragmentation, its shaping and its genetically engineered reproduction, a debate that links the past century to the new one, may lead the beholder facing the Finnish sculptor Heli Ryhänen's works to think, perhaps too readily, of a critical response from a feminist perspective to the contemporary cult of the body. The discourse of gender, after all, has insistently sought to deconstruct images of masculinity and femininity that had been constructed by patriarchal strategies.[1] The apologias of trans-human or a-human sciences permanently call for an artistic engagement of the body.

Die forcierte Virtualität der digitalen (Spiele-)Welt lässt uns unseren Körper potentiell als umfassend veränderbar erleben. Die Figurenkonstellationen Heli Ryhänens muten an wie *tableaux vivants*,[2] um ihren Anspruch auf Aktualität anzumelden und ihr Potential zu zeigen. Heli Ryhänen bezieht die Ausstellungssituation mit ein, sie schafft ein räumliches Ganzes. Dazu verwendet sie Wände aus transparenten Stoffen, Stoffe, die zu Gehäusen, Treppen, Paravents werden, denen die Einzelfigur oder die Gruppe zugeordnet wird. Die Rhythmisierung des Raumes beschränkt sich nicht auf Greifbares, auch mit Geräuschen oder der Spannung eines inszenierten Hell-Dunkels aus Kunstlicht gliedert die Künstlerin ihre Installationen. Solche inszenatorischen Elemente erinnern an die Videos, die Tony Oursler auf Kissen oder andere Gegenstände projiziert. Andeutungen von psychischen Zuständen und von Gefühlen sind ebenso klar wie sublim eingefangen. Nicht überraschend nennt sie Louise Bourgeois als beeindruckendes Vorbild ihrer Studienzeit. Der weibliche Blick geht stets auf ein Gegenüber; um in Rilkes Bild zu bleiben, konstatiert er das, was die Umrisslinie des Fühlens von außen prägt, wie eine Gussform den Gusskörper formt. Mit dem Titel *Out of the blur* beschreibt es die Künstlerin treffend – aus dem Amorphen taucht flüchtig ein Umriss auf, eine wolkige Gestalt, die unscharf bleibt, keine bloße Figur, sondern

The forceful virtuality of the digital (gaming) world enables us to experience our own bodies as potentially capable of comprehensive modification. The constellations of Heli Ryhänen's figures create *tableaux vivants*[2] that have descended from the history paintings of the nineteenth century's salons in order to stake their claim to contemporary relevance and display their potential. Heli Ryhänen's work draws on the particular exhibition situation to create a total environment. To this end, she uses walls made of transparent fabrics that form boxes, staircases, or screens to which an individual figure or group is assigned. The rhythmical structure she lends to the room is not limited to tangible elements; the artist also uses sounds or the tension inherent in the staged chiaroscuro of artificial light to organize her installations. Such theatrical elements recall the videos Tony Oursler projects onto pillows or other objects. Her art captures suggestions of psychological states and of feelings with clarity as well as sublimity. Not surprisingly, she mentions Louise Bourgeois as an artist whose work made a deep impression on her when she was a student. The female gaze always addresses a counterpart or, to remain within Rilke's image, it states what shapes the contour of feeling from outside the way a casting mold shapes the cast. The title *Out of the*

die Figur *und* ihre Verfasstheit, ein momenthafter Zustand, der seinen Zerfall bereits ankündigt. Eine wolkig-vage Gestalt, wie sie ein Kunstraucher zustande gebracht haben könnte, oder wie sie uns beim Bleigießen am Silvesterabend unterkommt. Räumlich inszenierte *tableaux vivants* als indirekter, ergo weiblicher Blick auf die unsichtbare Architektur des Fühlens, bedingt durch das Korsett der sogenannten Umstände, unsere persönlichen, sozialen Bindungen.
Heli Ryhänen hat sich in vielen Techniken erprobt. Ton und Keramik, Fiberglas und Stahl hat sie als Materialien verwendet, mit Bronze arbeitet sie hin und wieder immer noch. Ihre erste weiche Skulptur entstand 1996, weil statische Skulpturen sie nicht mehr genügend forderten. Die weiche Skulptur bietet ihr die Herausforderung, im jeweiligen Ausstellungskontext einen spannungsvollen Moment zu erleben. Denn eine weiche Skulptur hängt, fällt, steht nie exakt so wie einst im Atelier oder in der vorherigen Ausstellungssituation.

> "Ich will nicht diese halbgefüllten Masken, / lieber die Puppe. Die ist voll. Ich will / den Balg aushalten und den Draht und ihr / Gesicht aus Aussehn. Hier. Ich bin davor."
> Rainer Maria Rilke, *4. Duineser Elegie*

blur describes it felicitously—a fleeting outline emerges from amorphousness, a cloudy shape that remains hazy, not a mere figure but the figure *and* what constitutes it, a momentary state that already betokens its disintegration. A cloudy and vague shape of the sort an artistic smoker might have managed to create; or we might encounter it when we pour lead on New Year's Eve. A spatial mise-en-scène of *tableaux vivants* as an indirect—and hence feminine—gaze on the invisible architecture of feeling, conditioned by the strictures of what we call circumstances, our personal and social ties.
Heli Ryhänen has tried her hand in many techniques. She has used clay and ceramics, fiberglass and steel; bronze is a material she still works with on occasion. Her first soft sculpture was created in 1996 when static sculptures no longer seemed exacting enough to her. The soft sculpture creates the challenge for her to experience a moment filled with tension in the individual exhibition context. For a soft sculpture never hangs, falls, or stands exactly the way it did back in the studio or in an earlier exhibition situation.

> "I don't want these half-filled masks,/ the doll is better. It's full. I'll gladly stand/ the stuffed tor-

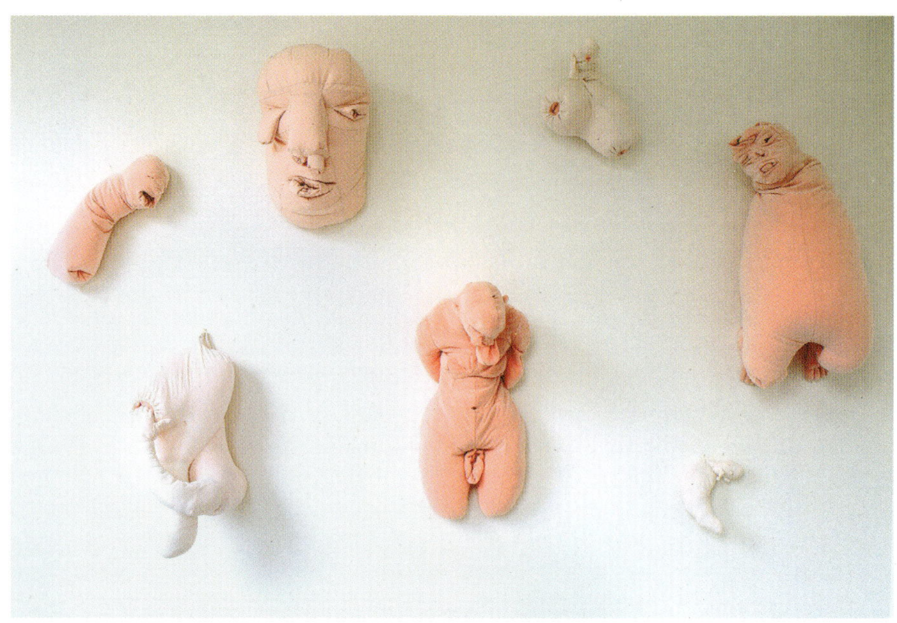

In-Out
2001
Stoff, Füllmaterial, mittlere Figur H 90 cm / fabric, fillings, figure in the middle 90 cm

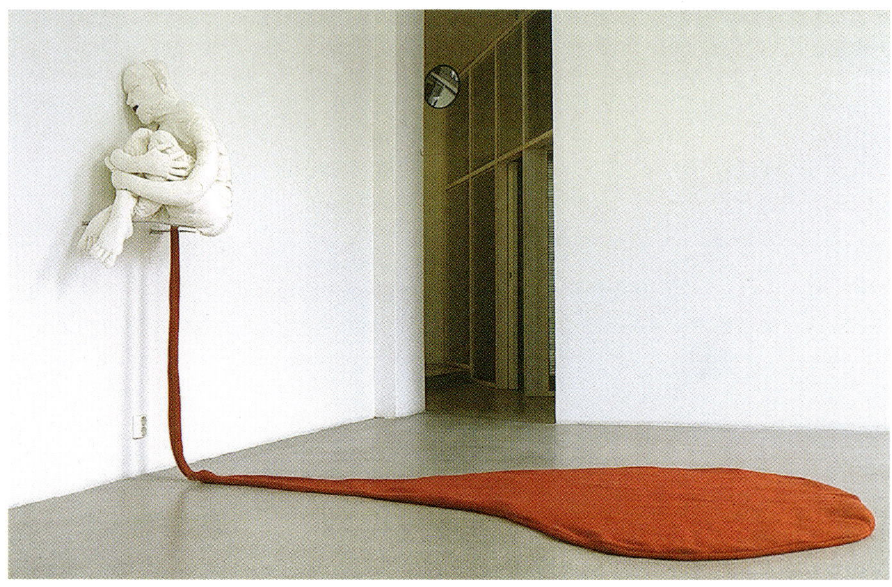

Pond
2001, Stoff, Filz, Figur / fabric, felt, figure, 50 x 60 x 80 cm, pond / Teich 300 cm

Das Überzeitliche der Puppe als Kunstfigur betont der Bildhauer Lothar Fischer: „Die lebendige Puppe, die ‚Kunstfigur', ist also autark und ein Gleichnis für den Menschen, ja sie stellt, wie auch die bildende Kunst im allgemeinen, eine Analogie zu seiner zweckfreien Existenz dar."[3]

Fischer sieht in ihr eine Kunstform parallel zur Natur. Obwohl er den Begriff Puppe verwendet, distanziert er sich gleichzeitig von der einschränkenden Begrifflichkeit, wenn damit lediglich die Simulation von Wirklichkeit gemeint ist. Bei der Kunstfigur schätzt Fischer die fantasievolle Vielgestaltigkeit.

Ausdrücklich bezieht sich Lothar Fischer auf Hans Bellmer, dessen ‚Poupée' eindeutig sexuell konnotiert ist.[4] Die Sexualisierung der Puppe, die eben eine Künstler- und keine Kinderpuppe ist, bringt das Unheimliche als verstörendes Ausdruckselement ein.

Hans Bellmer, der bei seiner ersten Nachkriegsausstellung in Berlin in der Person der Schriftstellerin Unica Zürn die Personifikation seiner Gliederpuppe zu erkennen glaubte, konstruierte oder entwarf seit 1933 seine Puppen, die er fotografisch inszenierte. Er verglich die ‚unmögliche' Kombinatorik von Puppen-Körperteilen mit Anagrammen und ihrem sinnstiftenden Zufallsprinzip. Aber das sexuelle Element der me-

so and the wire and its face/ made out of looks. Here. I'm right in front."

Rainer Maria Rilke, *Fourth Duino Elegy*

The sculptor Lothar Fischer emphasizes the transhistorical quality of the doll as an artificial character: "So the living doll, the 'artificial character,' is autarkic and a metaphor for man; more precisely, like the visual arts more generally, it represents an analogy of his purposeless existence."[3] Fischer regards the doll as a form of art that parallels nature. And although he uses the term "doll," he also distances himself from the limitations associated with this concept when it is used to describe the mere simulation of reality. What Fischer appreciates about the artificial character is its imaginative formal diversity.

Lothar Fischer explicitly refers to Hans Bellmer, whose *poupée* bears unambiguously sexual connotations.[4] The sexualization of the doll, now clearly an artist's and not a child's doll, introduces the uncanny as a disturbing expressive feature.

Hans Bellmer, who believed he had met the personification of his jointed doll when he encountered the writer Unica Zürn during his first postwar exhibition in Berlin, constructed or conceived his dolls since 1933 in photographic mises-en-scène. He compared the 'im-

chanischen Androiden des Erotomanen Bellmer[5] als eines Pygmalion des 20. Jahrhunderts besitzen dessen Puppen natürlich nicht exklusiv. Die Puppe, die Oskar Kokoschka 1918 als Surrogat für seine Geliebte Alma Mahler nach eigenen detaillierten Entwürfen herstellen ließ, war wenig subtil gedacht und letztlich eine Enttäuschung, und sie wurde schließlich zum Modell des Malers quasi herabgestuft, nachdem sie seine erotischen Anforderungen nicht erfüllen konnte,[6] um am Ende in einer festlich-bukolischen Inszenierung zerstört zu werden.

Auf sensible Art zurückhaltend sexuell konnotiert waren die Gliederpuppen, die Hannah Höch, Miterfinderin der Fotomontage, zwischen 1916 und 1918 anfertigte. Zwei davon konnte sie in den USA verkaufen, wo die Puppen auf Initiative der *Münchener Expressionistischen Werkstätten* ausgestellt waren. Bei der sogenannten Ersten Internationalen Dada-Messe in Berlin vom 1. Juli bis zum 25. August 1920 ließ sich Hannah Höch im Hof der Kunsthandlung Otto Burchard mit einer ihrer Puppen fotografieren: „Sie schlüpft nicht nur äußerlich in das gleiche Kostüm, reflektiert nicht nur theoretisch über das subtile Verhältnis Mensch und Puppe, sondern präsentiert sich vielmehr verpuppt, erstarrt in einer Beziehung, belebte Puppe und verpupptes Lebewesen, in einem Brennglas fixiert. Sich

possible' combinatorics of doll body parts to anagrams and their creation of meaning out of chance. Yet the sexual element in the mechanical androids created by Bellmer, an erotomaniac[5] and Pygmalion of the twentieth century, is of course not exclusive to these dolls. The doll Oskar Kokoschka had made in 1918 based on his own detailed sketches as a stand-in for his lover Alma Mahler was hardly subtle in conception and disappointing in reality; he ultimately degraded it after a fashion, using it as a model when it proved inadequate to his erotic demands,[6] and ended up destroying it in a festive-bucolic theatrical production.

The jointed dolls Hannah Höch, one of the inventors of photomontage, created between 1916 and 1918 carried more sensitive and restrained sexual overtones. She was able to sell two of them in the US, where the dolls were shown at an exhibition initiated by the *Munich Expressionist Workshops*. During the so-called First International Dada Fair held in Berlin between July 1 and August 25, 1920, Hannah Höch had her photograph taken with one of her dolls in the courtyard at Otto Burchard's art dealership: "Not only does she slip into the same outward costume, not only does she reflect on a theoretical level about the subtle relationship between human being and doll; more than that, she pres-

selbst erlebte Höch, wie sie einst bei einem Atelierabend auch in einer Satire vorträgt, als eine von Raoul Hausmann zerlegte Puppe, die wieder zusammenzufügen er nicht fähig wäre."[7]

> "...wenn mir zumut ist, / zu warten vor der Puppenbühne, nein, / so völlig hinzuschaun, daß, um mein Schauen / am Ende aufzuwiegen, dort als Spieler/ ein Engel hinmuß, der die Bälge hochreißt. / Engel und Puppe: dann ist endlich Schauspiel./ Dann kommt zusammen, was wir immerfort / entzwein, indem wir da sind. Dann entsteht / aus unsern Jahreszeiten erst der Umkreis/ des ganzen Wandelns. Über uns hinüber / spielt dann der Engel. [...]"
> Rainer Maria Rilke, *4. Duineser Elegie*

Die (Schaufenster-)Puppe war ein Fetisch-Objekt, das die Surrealisten gerne verwendeten, ein Schlüsselprotagonist. Wichtig war offenbar, dass alle künstlerischen Eingriffe vorgenommen wurden an einem teilweise gebrauchten Alltagsgegenstand, einem *objet trouvé*. Bekanntlich zeigte die große internationale Surrealismusausstellung 1938 in Paris eine „Straße der Puppen". Die groteske Wirkung als solche steht neben dem unabweisba-

ents herself as though pupated, frozen in interrelation, animated doll and pupated living being, fixed under a burning lens. As she herself contends on one occasion in a satirical appearance during an evening at the studio, Höch experienced herself as a doll Raoul Hausmann has dismembered and would be incapable of putting back together."[7]

> "... if I feel like it, / to wait before the puppet stage, no, / to gaze there so intensely that, to balance out/ my watching at the end, an angel must appear/ as actor there, who jerks the bodies up. / Angel and doll: then at last it's theater. / Then it comes together, what we split apart/ continually through our being here. Our seasons/ only then bring forth the sphere of the entire/ walk of life. The angel plays beyond / above us then. [...]"
> Rainer Maria Rilke, *Fourth Duino Elegy*

The doll, the (shop-window) mannequin was a fetish object the Surrealists liked to use, a key protagonist. What mattered, apparently, was that all artistic interventions would be performed on a partially used everyday object, an *objet trouvé*. The grand international Surrealist exhibition held in Paris in 1938, it is well known, featured a "street of

ren Bezug auf die Schöpfung, die Puppe oder die Marionette ist immer auch ein Homunculus, ein Wesen, das auf die Beseelung durch einen Schöpfer wartet und hofft. Wenn sie nicht wie bei *Balancing* oder *The Wait* an Hilfsmitteln (einer Schaukel, an Stäben wie bei einem Mobile) montiert sind, hängen die Figuren Ryhänens oft an Fäden oder Schnüren, weisen somit auf einen abwesenden übermenschlichen Puppenspieler, der sie in der nächsten Minute zum Spiel, d.h. zum Leben, erweckt: Der Spieler als Engel, der die Bälge hochreißt (Rilke).

Der Doppelcharakter, wie er auch in der Klage Hannah Höchs zur Selbstbeschreibung wird, zieht uns an. Die Puppe ist Möglichkeit und Sinnbild, ist Erdklumpen, Golem, Cyborg, Surrogat oder Idol – die Venus von Willendorf ist nicht weit. Mit ihr spielen wir den Kreator, und zugleich birgt sie das Unheimliche, droht sie doch, sich zu verselbständigen, uns und unsere Fantasien zu beherrschen. Heli Ryhänen reklamiert für sich, dass ihre räumlichen Figuren-Bilder auf tatsächlichen Beobachtungen beruhen, dass sie einerseits zeitlose Fragen aufwirft, existentielle Situationen heraufbeschwört, und andererseits unterschiedlichste reale Lebenssituationen schildert. Sie sucht vertraute Konstellationen aus dem Spektrum der zwischenmenschlichen Beziehungen, aber sie bewegt sich auch auf die Grenze zu,

dolls." The grotesque impression these objects make by themselves stands next to their irrefutable relation to creation; the doll or puppet is always also a homunculus, a being waiting and hoping to be brought to life by a creator. When they are not mounted to supports such as a swing or rods resembling a mobile, as in *Balancing* or *The Wait*, Ryhänen's figures are often suspended from threads or strings, pointing to an absent superhuman puppeteer who will awaken them into play—that is, into life—the very next minute: the player as the angel who jerks the bodies up (Rilke).

The double nature also apparent in Hannah Höch's plaintive self-description appeals to us. The doll is possibility and symbol, is a golem, a cyborg, a surrogate or idol—the Venus of Willendorf is not far off. We play creators with it, while it also harbors the uncanny, for it threatens to take on a life of its own, to dominate us and our fantasies. Heli Ryhänen's claim is that her spatial figural images are based on actual observation; that she raises timeless questions, invokes existential situations, while also depicting a variety of real-life situations. She seeks out familiar constellations from the spectrum of human relationships, but she also feels her way toward the boundary separating consciousness from subconscious, waking from dream. The 'nakedless' nakedness of

die das Bewusstsein und das Unterbewusste, Wachheit und Traum trennt. Die ‚nacktlose' Nacktheit von Ryhänens gepolsterten Stofffiguren bewirkt, dass sie paradoxerweise ein Stück weit ungegenständlich wirken – traumhaft-unwirklich. Überraschende Konstellationen der Figuren und so noch nicht gesehene Verzerrungen, wie sie ähnlich Hans Bellmer für seine Fotografien mit seiner Gelenkpuppe schuf und die Cindy Sherman auf ihre Art nachstellte, verunsichern den Betrachter, provozieren ihn zum Nachdenken.[8] Die Puppe als „Schauplatz von Fantasmen der Ganzheit und Zerstückelung."[9]
Heli Ryhänens Arbeit steht in einem polaren Verhältnis zu der eines Duane Hanson. Ihre inszenierten Figurenkonstellationen haben nichts Illustratives. Vielmehr verweisen sie mit poetischer Stringenz auf das Sinnbildhafte der Puppe *und* das einer puppenhaften Existenz. Assoziationen an ein kindliches Marionetten- oder Puppentheater erleiden Schiffbruch. Es ist stattdessen der Schock, der aus dem Vergleich des Lebens mit einem Puppendrama erwächst, die Erschütterung, die uns befällt, wenn wir die Marionette als Symbol unserer Existenz erkennen, wie es vor zwei Jahrhunderten Heinrich von Kleist in seinem Text *Über das Marionettentheater* vorexerziert hat. Die dort gestellte überzeitliche Frage ist die nach dem Verhältnis zwischen Vernunft und Gefühl. Eine quasi archaische

Ryhänen's padded fabric figures paradoxically makes them seem a bit un-objective—dreamlike and unreal. Surprising constellations of figures and contortions we have not seen before, not unlike the ones Hans Bellmer created for his photographs with his jointed doll, which Cindy Sherman reenacted in her own fashion, unsettle the beholder, provoking him to reflect.[8] The doll as a "site of phantasms of wholeness and dismemberment."[9]
Heli Ryhänen's work is the polar antagonist of, say, Duane Hanson's. There is nothing illustrative about her staged constellations of figures. Instead, they point, with poetic cogency, toward the symbolic character of the doll *and* that of a doll-like existence. Associations of childish puppetry or toy theater founder. Here, rather, is the shock we suffer from the comparison of life to a puppet drama, the jarring realization that comes over us when we recognize in the puppet a symbol of our existence, as Heinrich von Kleist demonstrated two centuries ago in his text *Concerning the Puppet Theater*. The timeless question he raises concerns the relationship between reason and feeling. A positively archaic problem we merely reencounter in different form in the virtual entanglements of a digitalized environment. In 1931, the Austrian writer Egon Friedell's *Cultural His-*

Problemstellung, die uns in den virtuellen Verwicklungen einer digitalisierten Umwelt nur neu begegnet. 1931 brachte der österreichische Schriftsteller Egon Friedell in seiner *Kulturgeschichte der Neuzeit* das Beispielgebende der menschlichen Puppenexistenz auf folgenden, von Demut geprägten Nenner:
"Treten wir nämlich nur ein wenig zurück, so bemerken wir, daß der Glaube, wir selbst seien die Urheber unserer körperlichen und seelischen Gesten, auf einer optischen Täuschung beruht: eine erhabene geheime Kraft, die unser ganzes Dasein in allen seinen großen und kleinen Bewegungen lenkt, wir könnten sie den unsichtbaren Dichter unseres Lebens nennen, wirkt sich auf dieser unserer Erdenbühne aus, und unter einem solchen Aspekt beginnt sich alles sogleich viel unpathetischer und unpersönlicher zu vollziehen."[10]
Mit ihren Inszenierungen aus weichen, figürlichen Skulpturen aktualisiert Heli Ryhänen die Frage nach dem freien Willen und der Bedingtheit unserer Existenz, die Frage nach der Vertauschbarkeit der Rollenmuster und die nach unseren persönlichen Spielräumen.

Hans-Peter Miksch

[1] In der deutschen Synchronisation des Filmes *Haben und Nichthaben* mit Lauren Bacall und Humphrey Bogart (1944, Regie Howard Hawks) ruft der Protagonist seine Filmpartnerin permanent „Puppe", währenddessen sie ihn beharrlich „Chief" nennt. Mann und Frau als Chef und Puppe. Das Synonym „Puppe" für eine begehrenswerte Frau bürgerte sich in England vor 1864 ein. In den USA geschah das erst um 1930 ff. (vergl. Jon Stratton, *Man-Made Women*. Aus: *The Desirable Body: Cultural fetishism and the erotics of consumption*. Manchester University Press, 1996).
[2] Lebende Bilder.
[3] Lothar Fischer (1933–2004), *Zur Kunst aus bildnerischer Sicht*. 8. Kapitel, S. 46. Waakirchen, 2001.
[4] Er war längst nicht der einzige Künstler, der sich auf Hans Bellmer (1902–1975) bezog. Auch die Fotokünstlerin Cindy Sherman hat sich selbst für eine Aufnahme in die Puppe Bellmers verwandelt, um diesen Aspekt einer künstlerischen Sichtweise auf die Frau als Objekt zu kommentieren und zu erweitern, weil ihre ‚Puppe' männliche und weibliche Genitalien haben kann.
[5] Gottfried Sello in einer Kritik der Bellmer-Retrospektive in Hannover 1967: *Kunst und Erotik sind für ihn identisch*. "Die Zeit", 19. Ausgabe, 1967.
[6] Vgl. www.alma-mahler.com; Kokoschka hätte wohl eher ein Angebot geholfen, wie man es in den USA heutigen Tages findet („*RealDoll*").
[7] Julia Dech, *Sieben Blicke auf Hannah Höch*. Hamburg, 2002, S. 34.
[8] Heli Ryhänen, unveröffentlichtes, undatiertes Manuskript: „The unforeseen elements and surprising nuances or distortions bring something unsettling and thought-provoking into the work of art."
[9] Sigrid Schade, *Die Medien/Spiele der Puppe - Vom Mannequin zum Cyborg. Das Interesse aktueller Künstlerinnen und Künstler am Surrealismus*. www.medienkunstnetz.de (Stand 24.1.2011).
[10] E.F., *Kulturgeschichte der Neuzeit*, Ungekürzte Sonderausgabe in einem Band, München 1979, S. 1471.

tory of the Modern Age summed up the exemplary character of the human puppet-existence in the following words suffused with humility:

"If we step back ever so little, we shall see that the belief that we ourselves are the originators of our bodily and spiritual gestures rests upon an optical delusion. A great secret force which guides our whole existence in all its movements, great and small—we might call it the invisible poet of our life—works itself out on this our earthly stage; and seen under such an aspect, everything begins at once to accomplish itself in a far more unemotional and impersonal way."[10]

Heli Ryhänen's mise-en-scène of soft figural sculptures raises old questions in a new way: questions regarding free will and the conditions determining our existence, regarding the exchangeability of role-patterns and our own personal freedoms.

Hans-Peter Miksch

[1] In the movie *To Have and Have Not* starring Lauren Bacall and Humphrey Bogart (1944, directed by Howard Hawks), the protagonist steadily calls his costar "doll," to which she persistently responds by calling him "chief." Man and woman as chief and doll: in England, the word "doll" came into use as a synonym for a desirable woman before 1864, but in the US this process did not take place around or after 1930 (cf. John Stratton, "Man-Made Women," in *The Desirable Body: Cultural Fetishism and the Erotics of Consumption*, Manchester: Manchester University Press, 1996).

[2] I.e., living images.

[3] Lothar Fischer (1933–2004), *Zur Kunst aus bildnerischer Sicht*, Waakirchen: Oreos, 2001, ch. 8, p. 46.

[4] He was by far not the only artist drawing on the work of Hans Bellmer (1902–1975). In one picture, the photographer Cindy Sherman has transformed herself into the Bellmerian doll in order to respond to this aspect of an artistic perspective on woman as an object and expand it: her 'doll' possesses male and female genitals.

[5] As Gottfried Sello wrote in a review of the 1967 Bellmer retrospective in Hanover: "Art and eroticism, to him, are identical." *Die Zeit*, no. 19 (1967).

[6] Cf. www.alma-mahler.com; Kokoschka would probably have been better served with a doll of the sort one can nowadays buy in the US ("*RealDoll*").

[7] Julia Dech, *Sieben Blicke auf Hannah Höch*, Hamburg, 2002, 34.

[8] As Heli Ryhänen puts it in an unpublished and undated manuscript: "The unforeseen elements and surprising nuances or distortions bring something unsettling and thought-provoking into the work of art."

[9] Sigrid Schade, "Die Medien/Spiele der Puppe – Vom Mannequin zum Cyborg. Das Interesse aktueller Künstlerinnen und Künstler am Surrealismus," www.medienkunstnetz.de (January 24, 2011).

[10] Egon Friedell, *A Cultural History of the Modern Age*, vol. 3: *The Crisis of the European Soul from the Black Death to the World War*, trans. Charles Francis Atkinson, New York: Knopf, 1964, p. 440.

Heli Ryhäsen installaatiot eivät *tableaux vivants* -töiden tapaan vaikuta maalatuilta kuvilta, vaan kuvanveistäjä on ottanut käytettävissä olevan tilan ja tilanteen mukaan. Se rytmittää näyttelytilaa ja lavastaa sitä lisäksi äänillä tai valolla. Näyttelyn nimellä *Out of the Blur* kuvanveistäjä hahmottaa pehmeiden veistosten vaikutusta, niiden kuin unesta tai sumusta nousevaa läsnäoloa: naisen näkökulmasta sosiaaliseen vastakkaisuuteen syntyy tunnelmien, mielentilojen arkkitehtuuria. R. M. Rilken neljättä Duinon elegiaa mukaillen se, *mikä muovaa tuntemisen ääriviivat*, tulee näkyviin. Nukke kuuluu taidehistorian perinteeseen yhtä lailla taideteoksen hahmona kuin seksuaalisena fetissinä surrealistisine mahdollisuuksineen. Nukke on muun muassa korvike, idoli, Golem-hahmon tai kotihengettären kaltainen olento; marionettina se on myös vertauskuva. Heli Ryhänen taikoo esiin eksistentiaalisia tilanteita, hän tekee tietoisuuden ja alitajunnan rajalla liikkuvia asetelmia. Katsoja löytää itsensä jälleen olemassaolonsa suhteellisuutta, roolimalleja ja niiden vaihdettavuutta sekä henkilökohtaista liikkumavaraansa koskettavien arkaaisten ja ajattomien kysymysten ääreltä. Vaikka monilla elämänaloilla yhä voimistuvan digitaalisen maailman virtuaalisuuden perusteella voidaan ajatella, että kehomme on kokonaisuudessaan muokattavissa, ajatuksen hämmentävyys ei silti ole kovinkaan kaukana todellisuudestamme.

Hans-Peter Miksch

Werke / Works

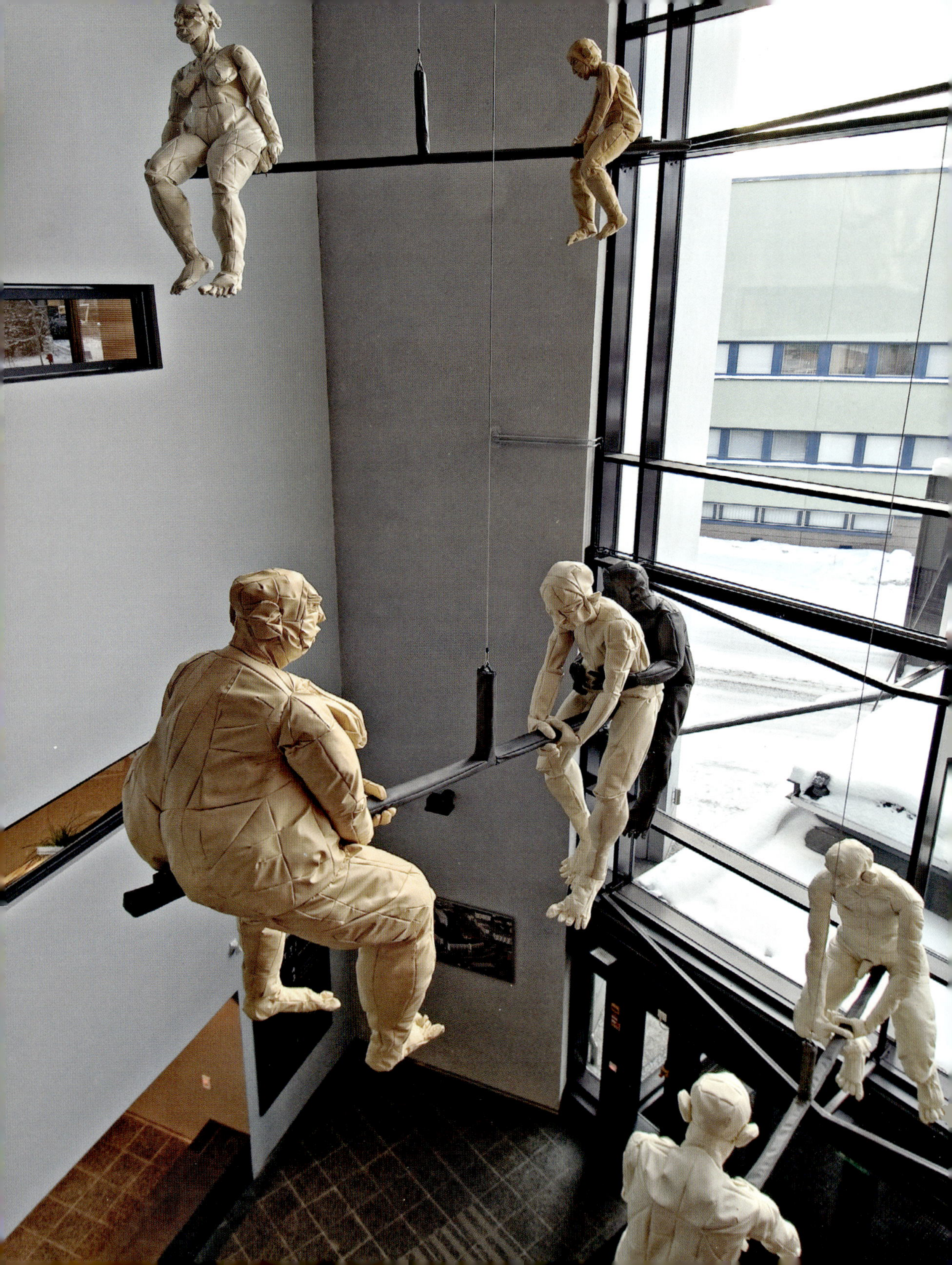

Balancing
Installation, 2010
Kunstleder, Stahl, Füllmaterial / artificial leather, steel, fillings
Ankauf / Commissioned work, Tax and Employment office Sinetti,
Jyväskylä, Finnland / Finland
Foto / Photo Pekka Helin

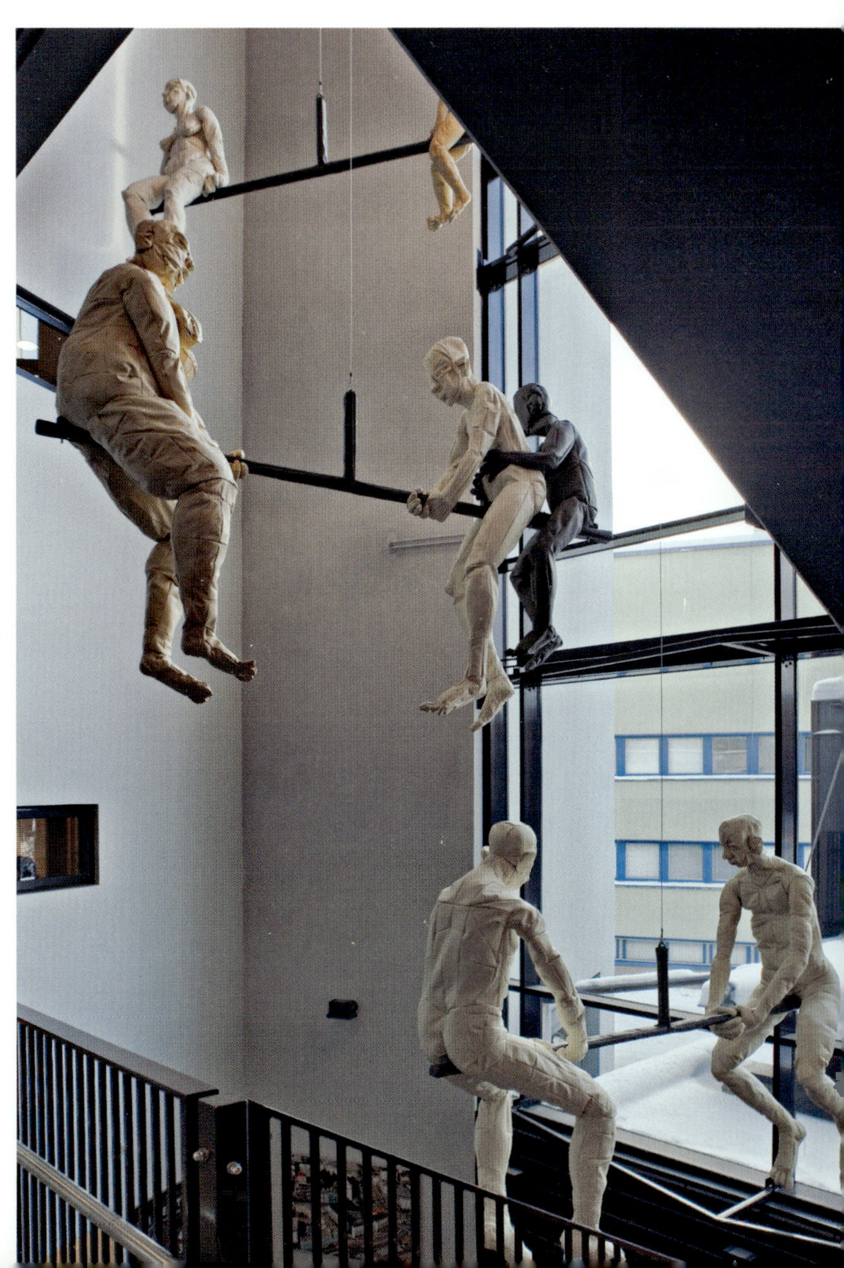

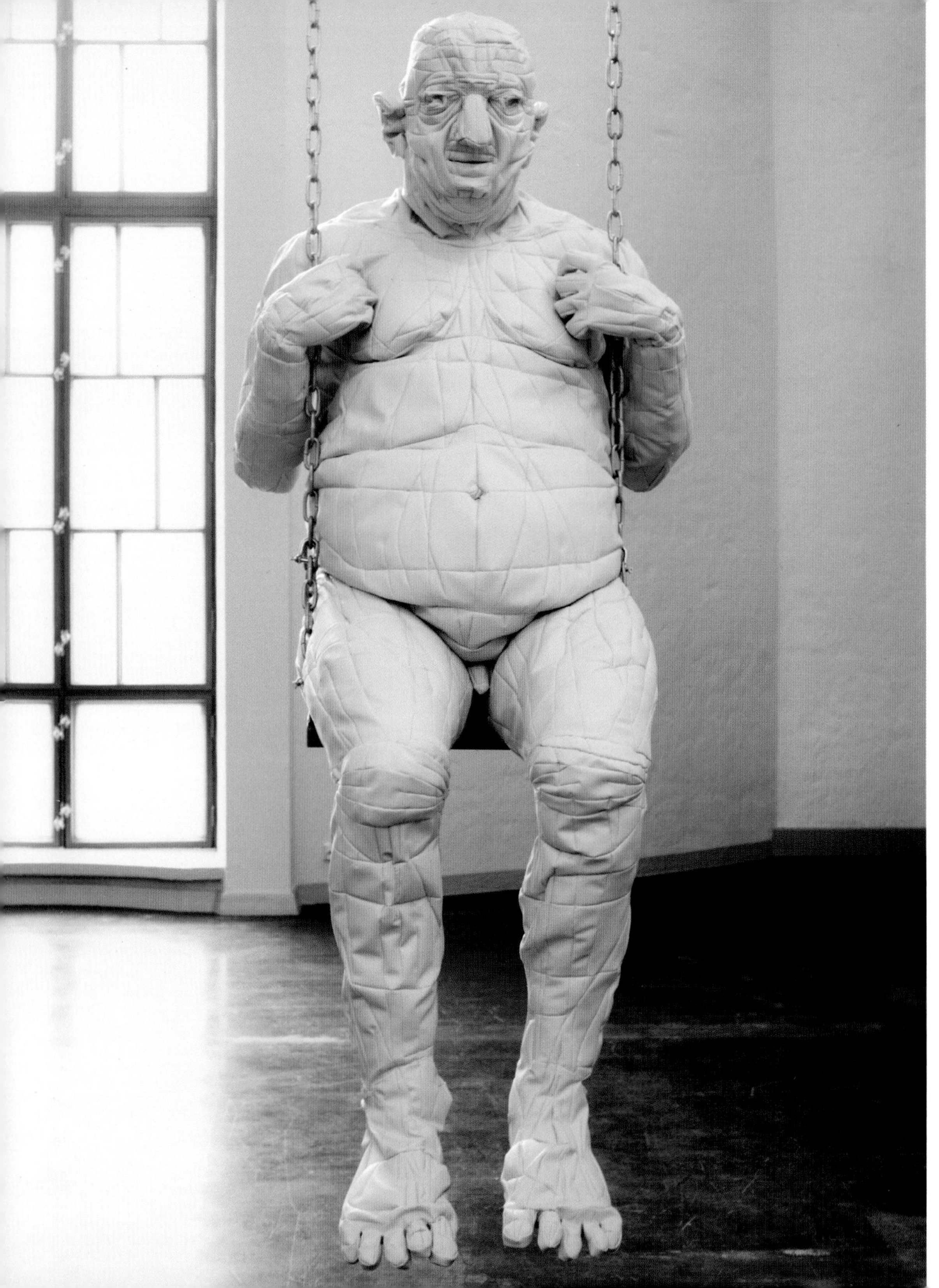

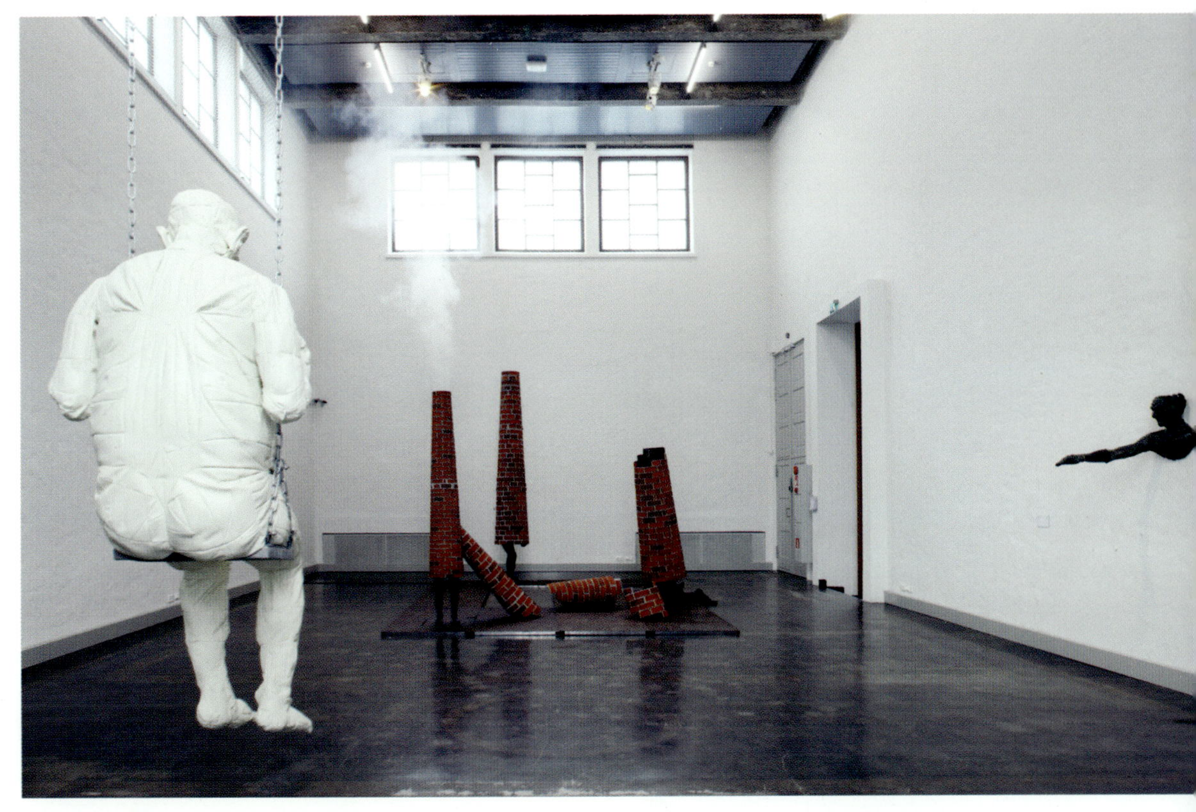

Slow motion
2010
Kunstleder, Stahl, Füllmaterial, Kette / artificial leather, steel, fillings, chain
270 x 90 x 130 cm
Foto / Photo Patrik Rastenberger

Preservation
2010
Bronze / bronze, 40 x 50 x 90 cm
Foto / Photo Patrik Rastenberger

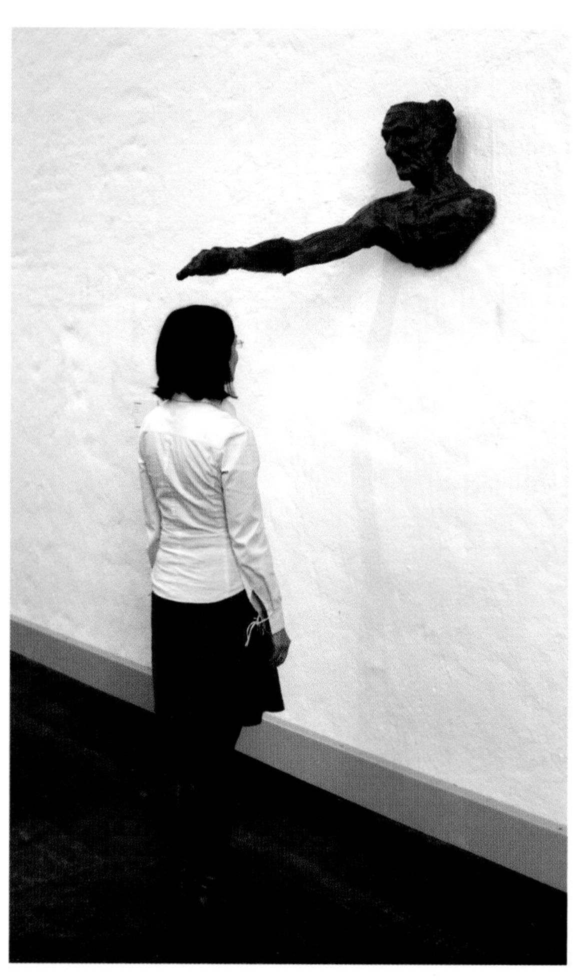

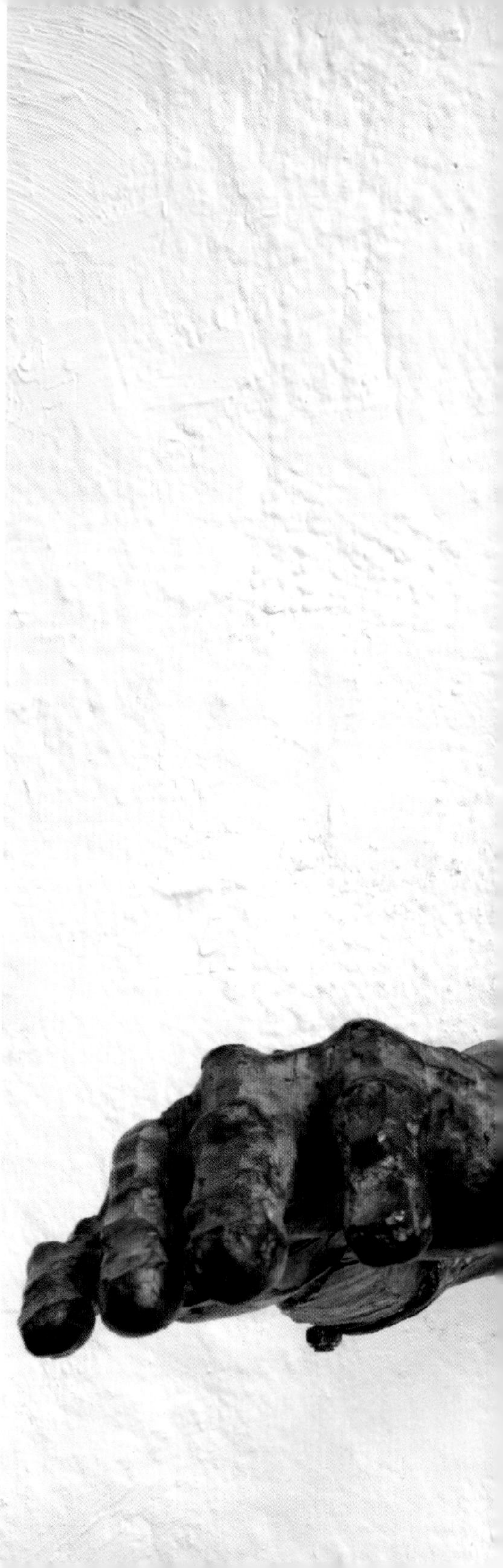

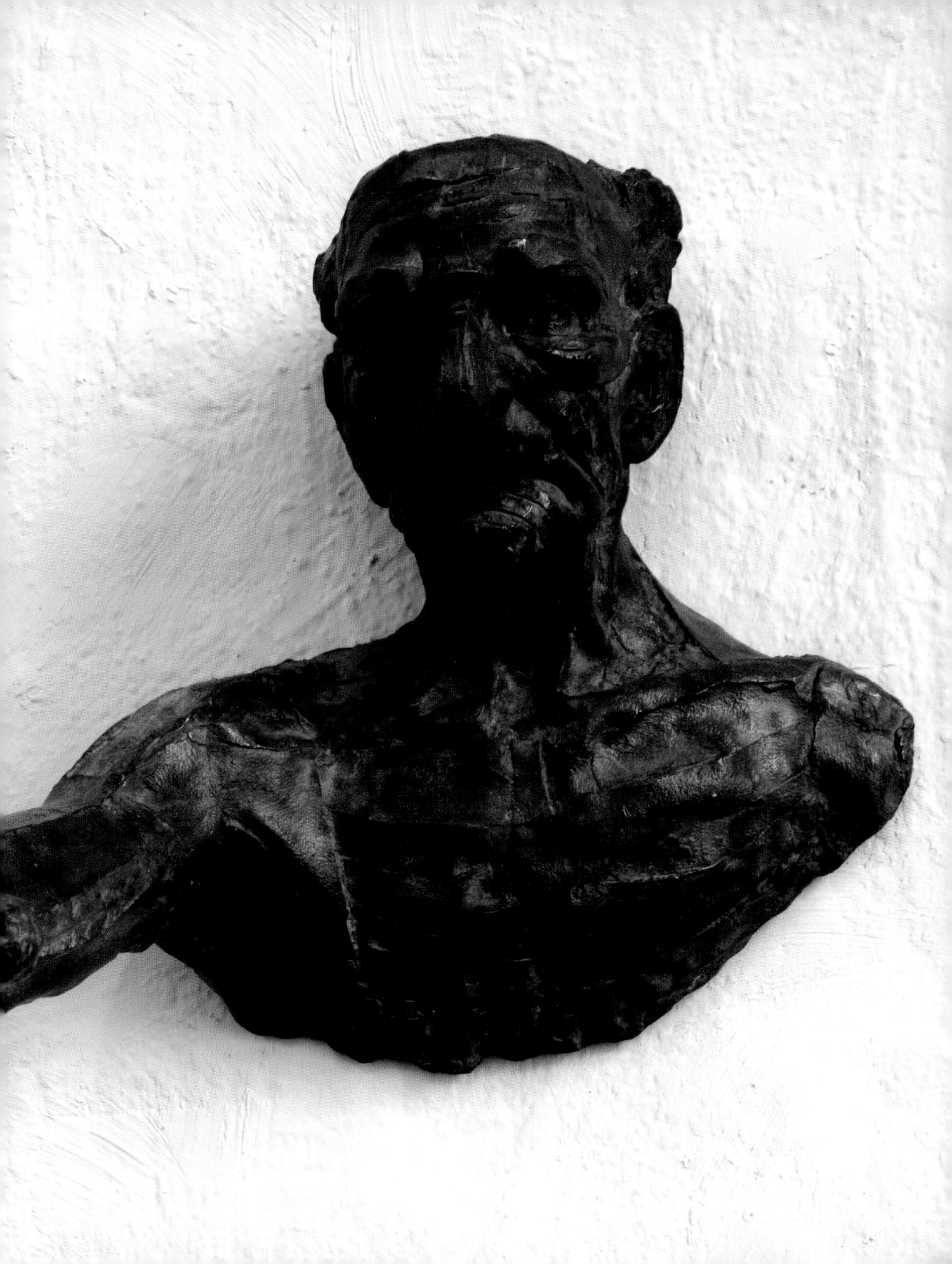

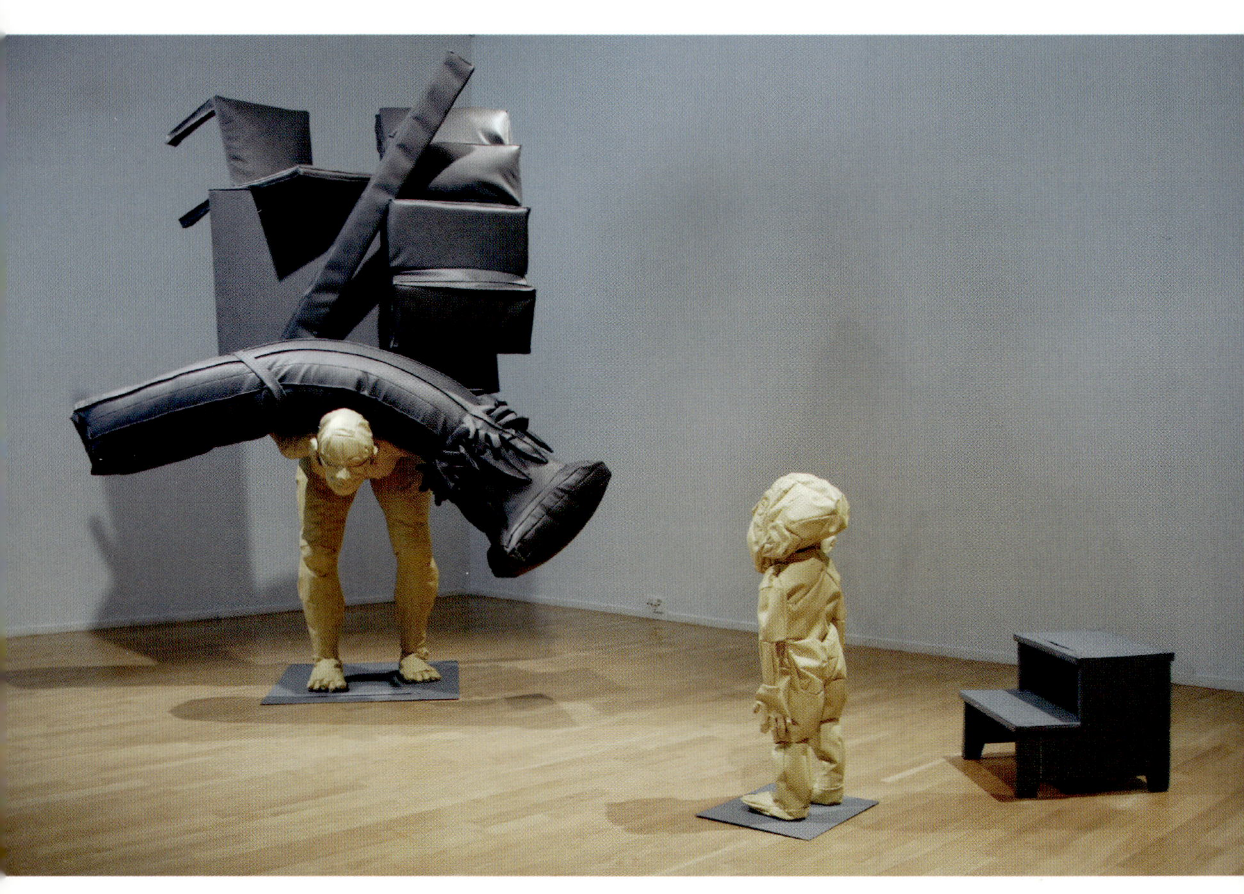

History repeating
Installation, 2009
Kunstleder, Stahl, Füllmaterial, Holz / artificial leather, steel, fillings, wood

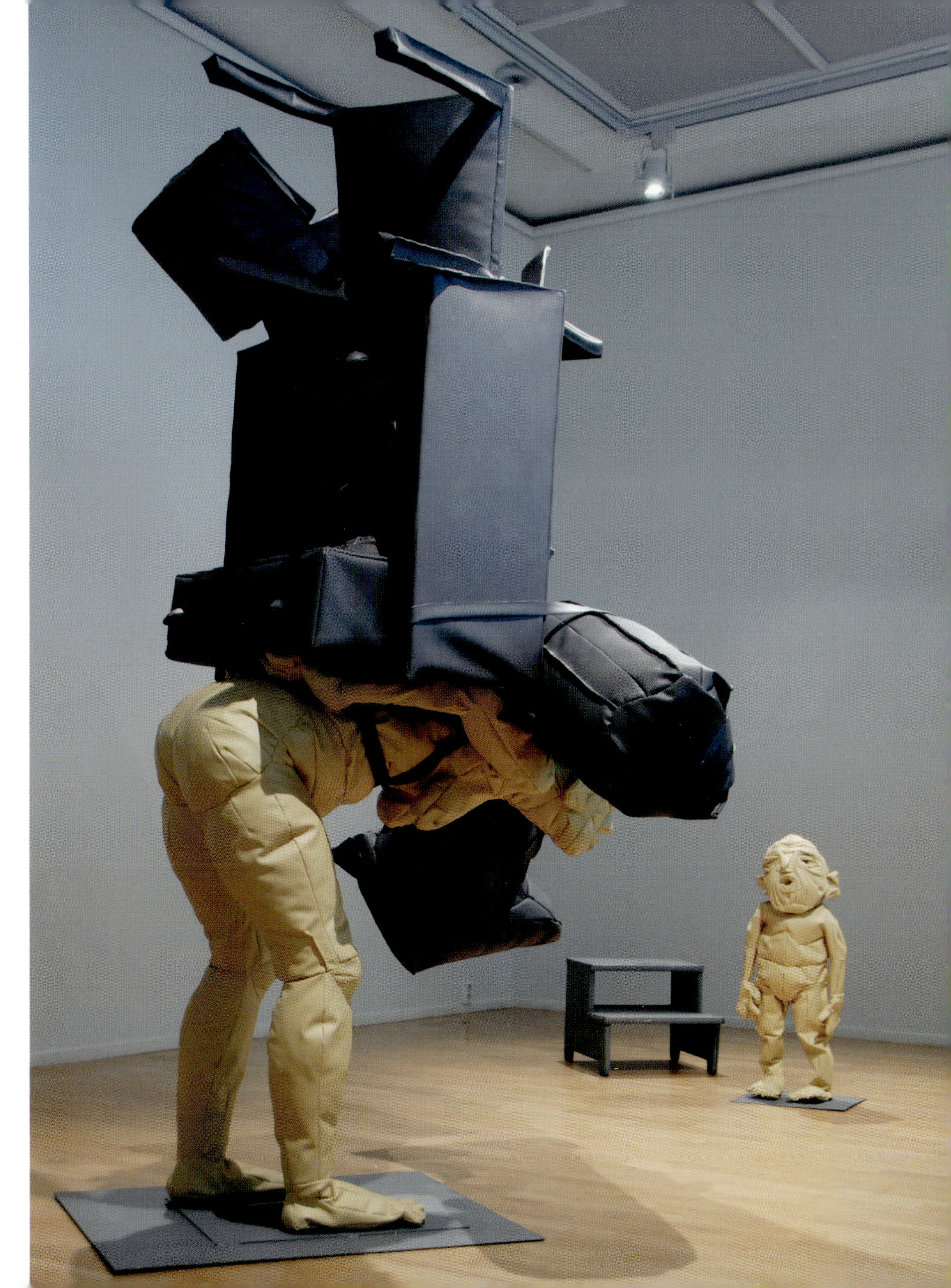

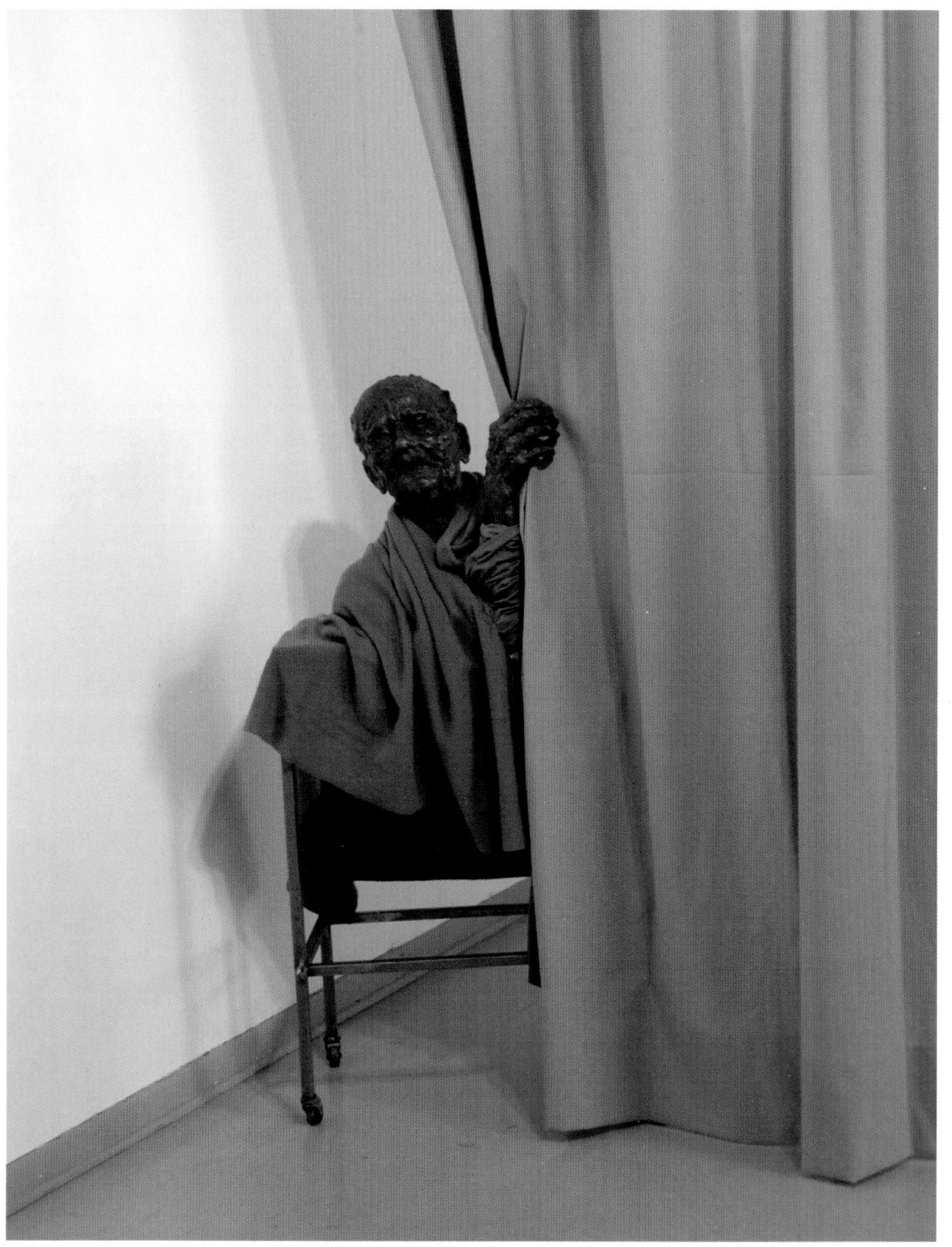

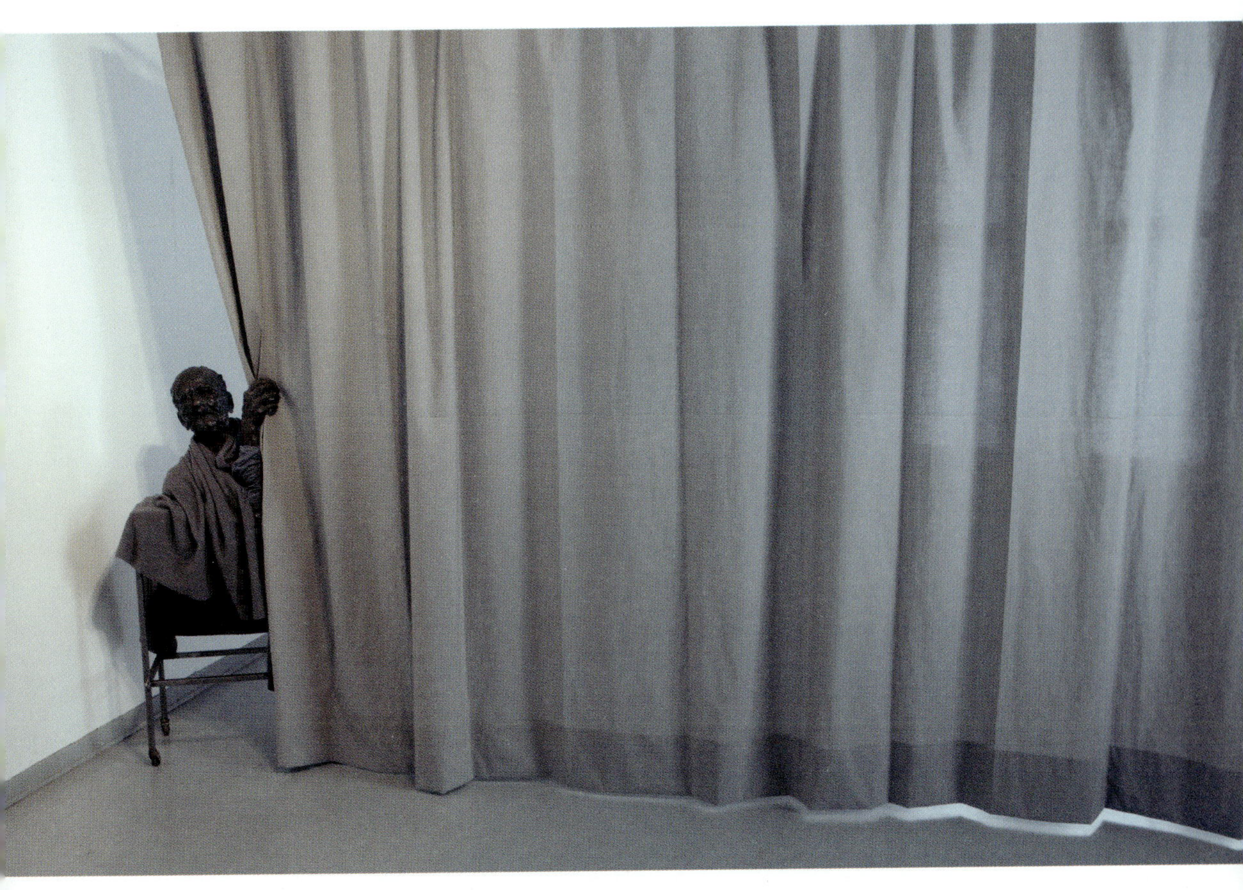

Farewell
Installation, 2009
Bronze, Stahl, Stoff / bronze, steel, fabric

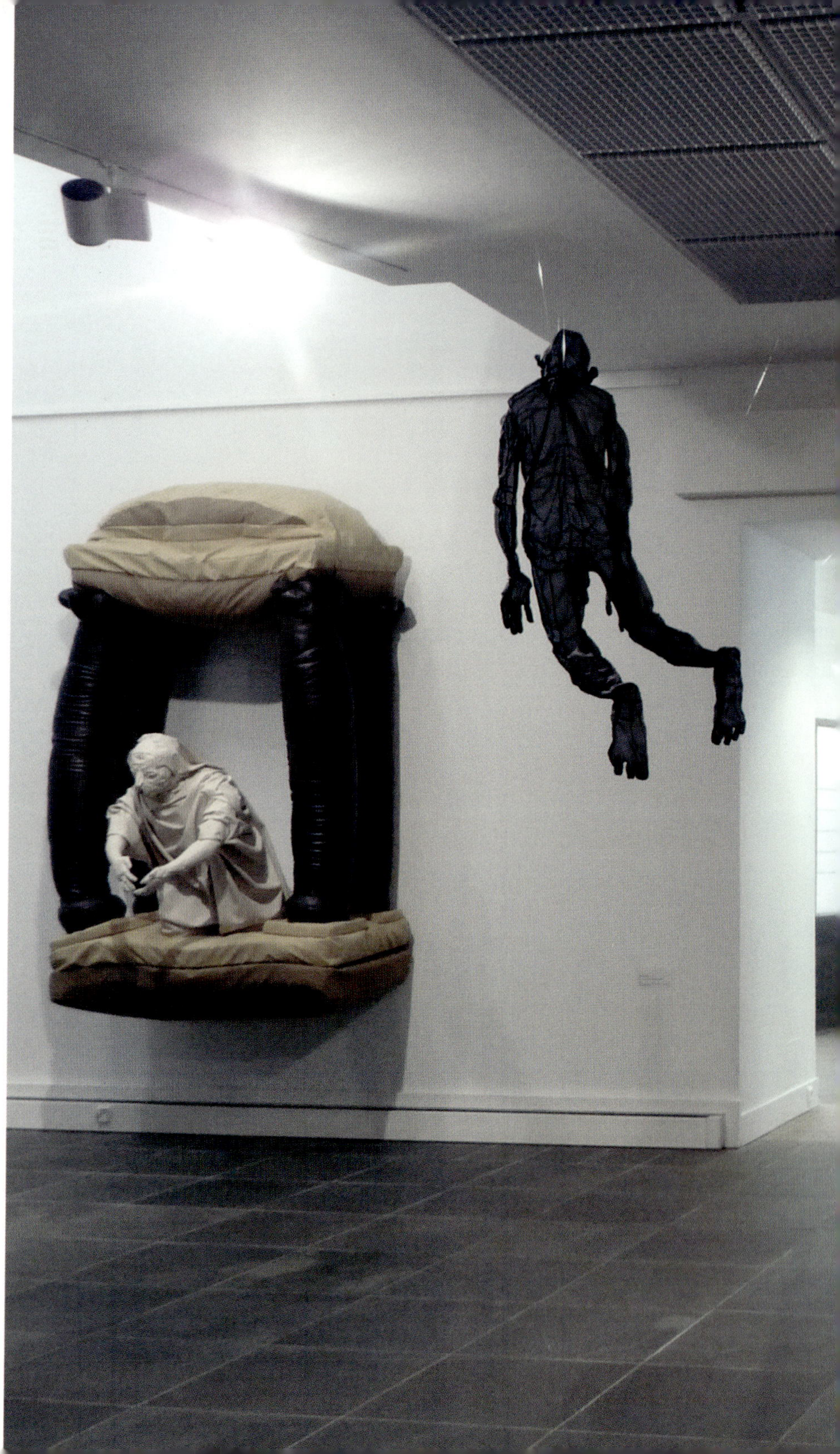

Another Frequency
Installation, 2009
Stoff / fabric

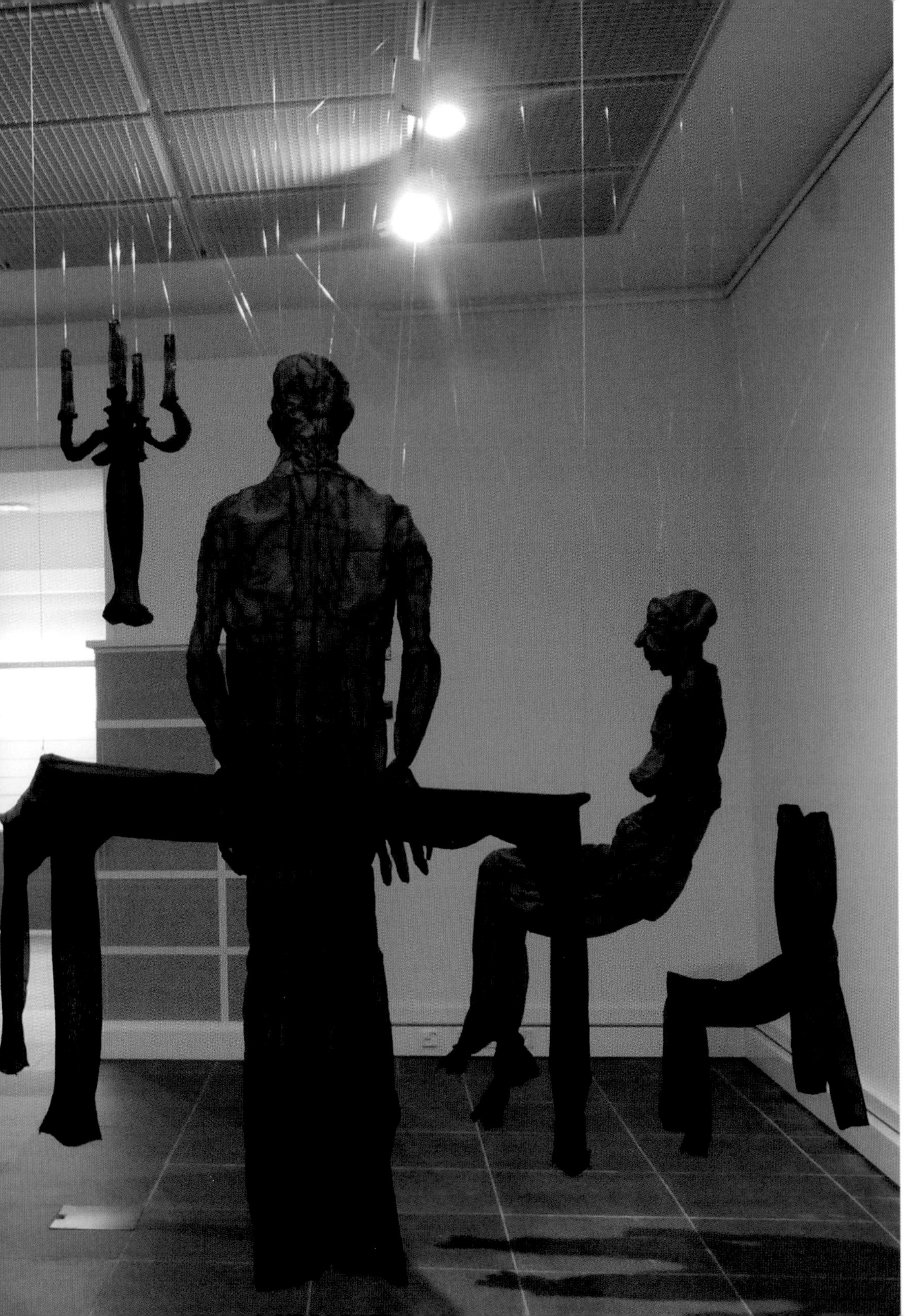

Another Frequency
Detail / detail

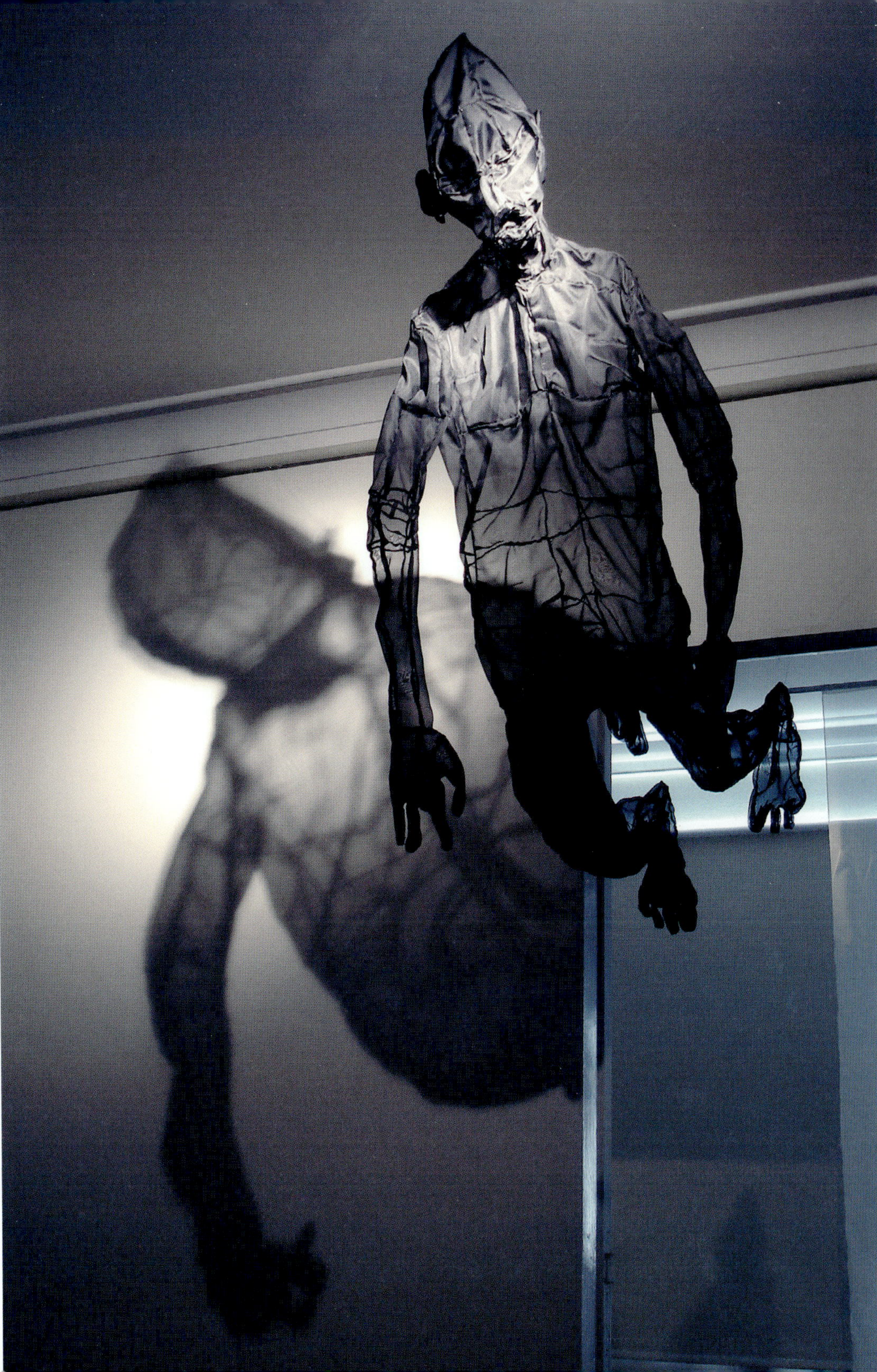

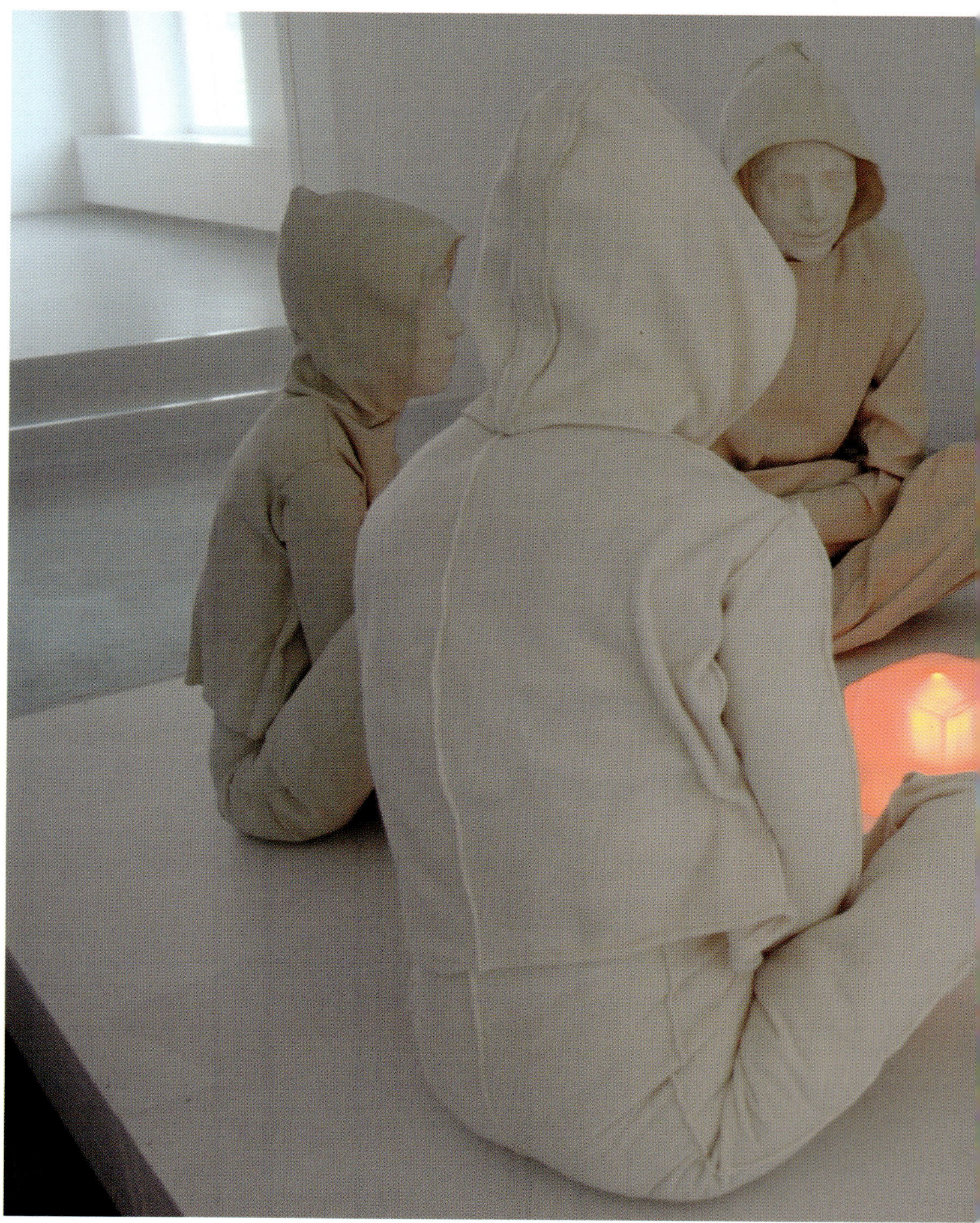

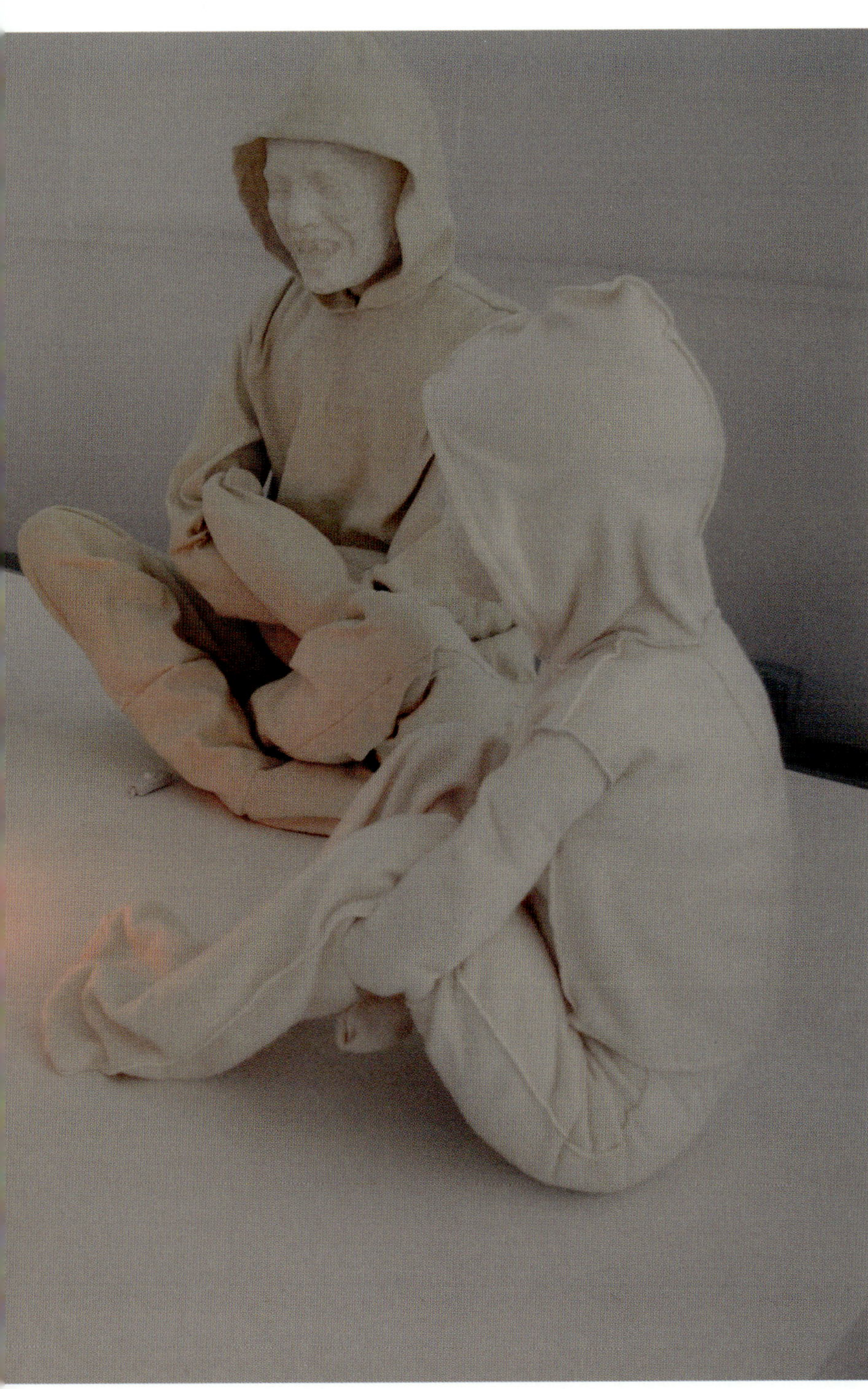

Evil Shepherd
Installation, 2007
Papiermaché, Stoff, Stahl, Füllmaterial, farbiges Licht /
paper mâché, fabric, steel, fillings, coloured light

Encapsulation
2007
Künstliches Fell, Stoff, Füllmaterial / artificial fur, fabric, fillings
125 x 150 x 60 cm

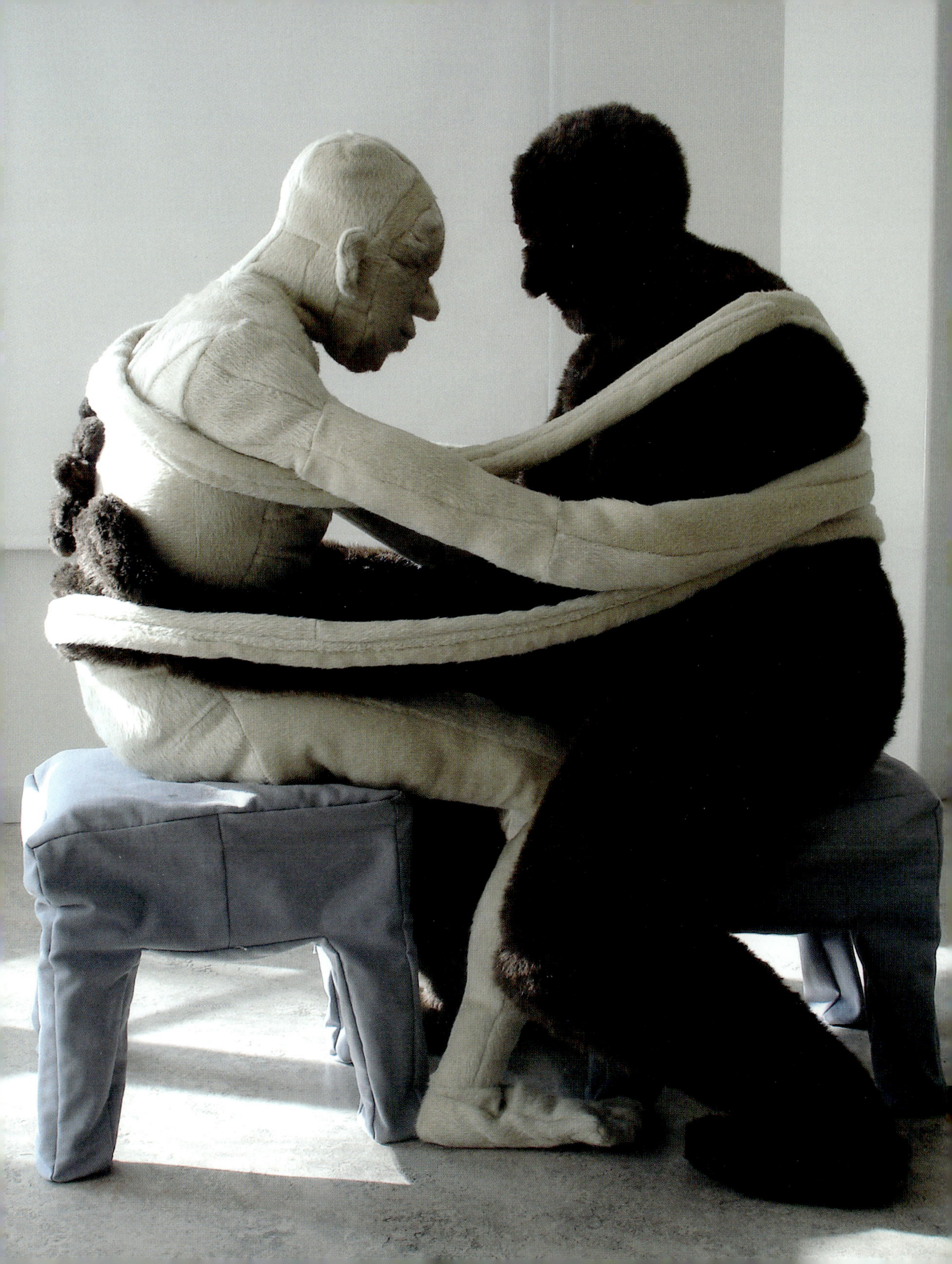

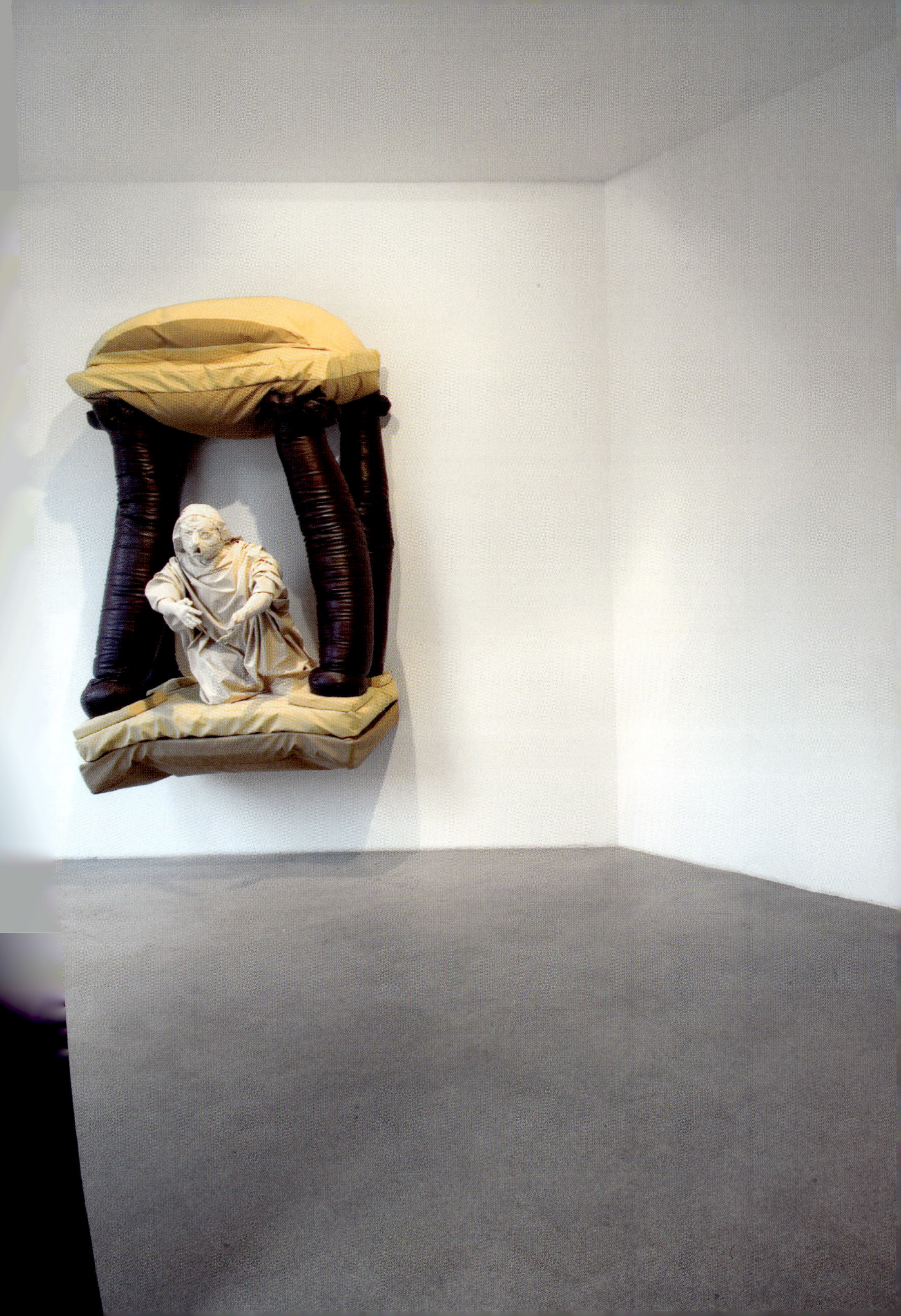

Connection in confidence
2007
Kunstleder, Stahl, Füllmaterial / artificial leather, steel, fillings
300 x 150 x 100 cm, 55 x 30 x 15 cm
Foto / Photo Jussi Tiainen

The Wait
Installation, 2006
Stoff, Stahl, Licht / fabric, steel, spotlight
Foto / Photo Ilari Järvinen

Auf den nächsten Seiten /
On the following pages
The Wait
Detail / detail

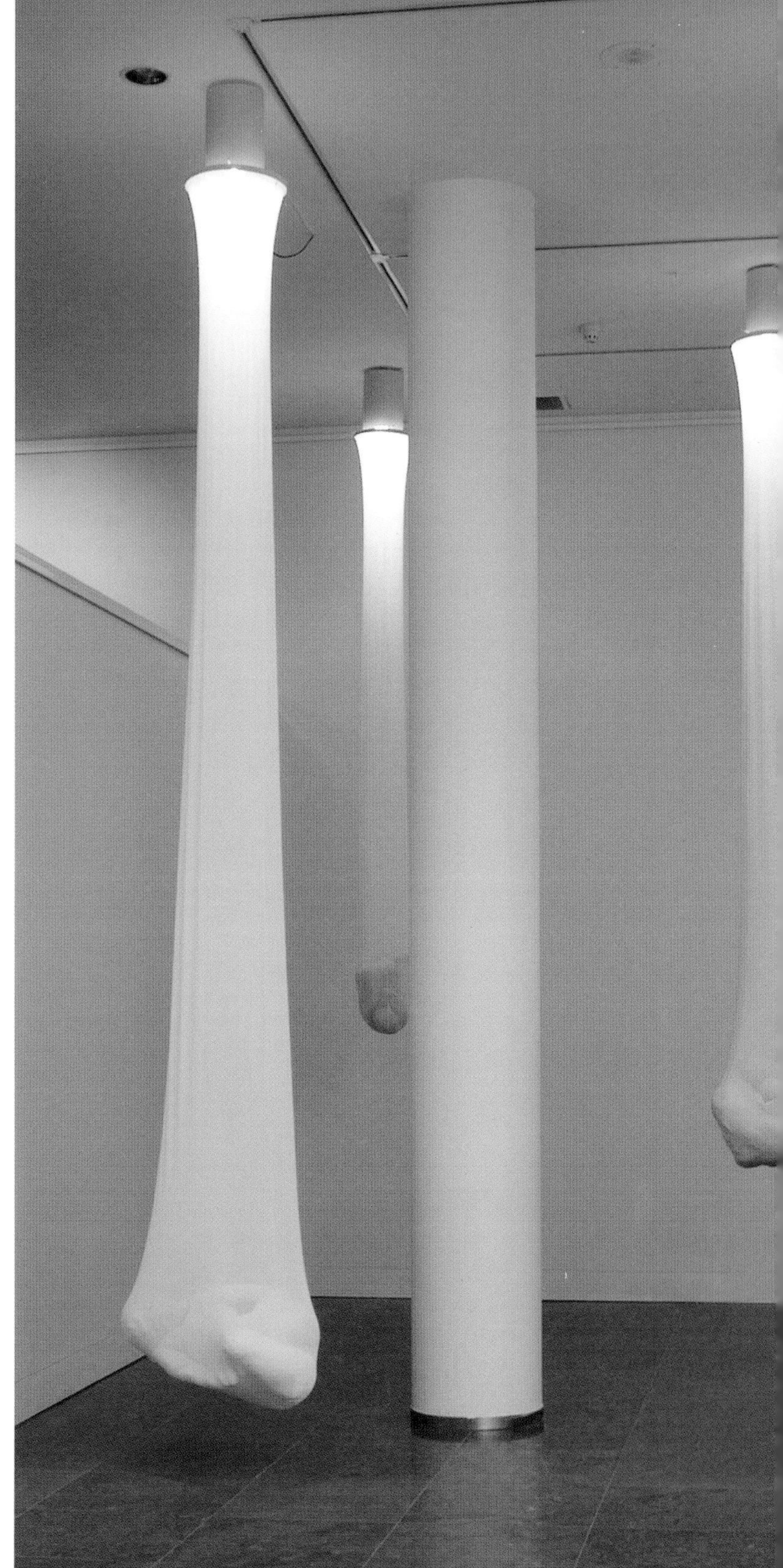

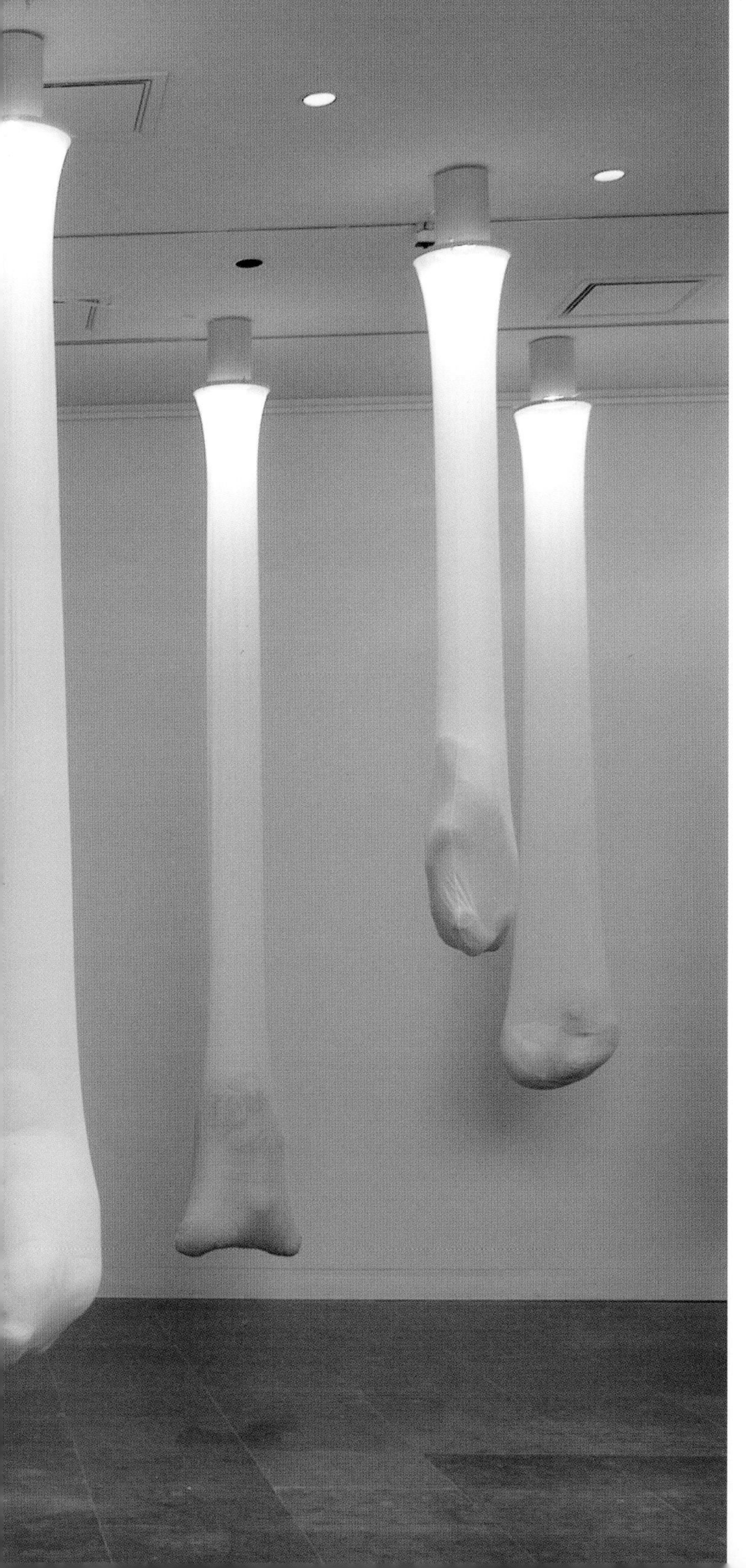

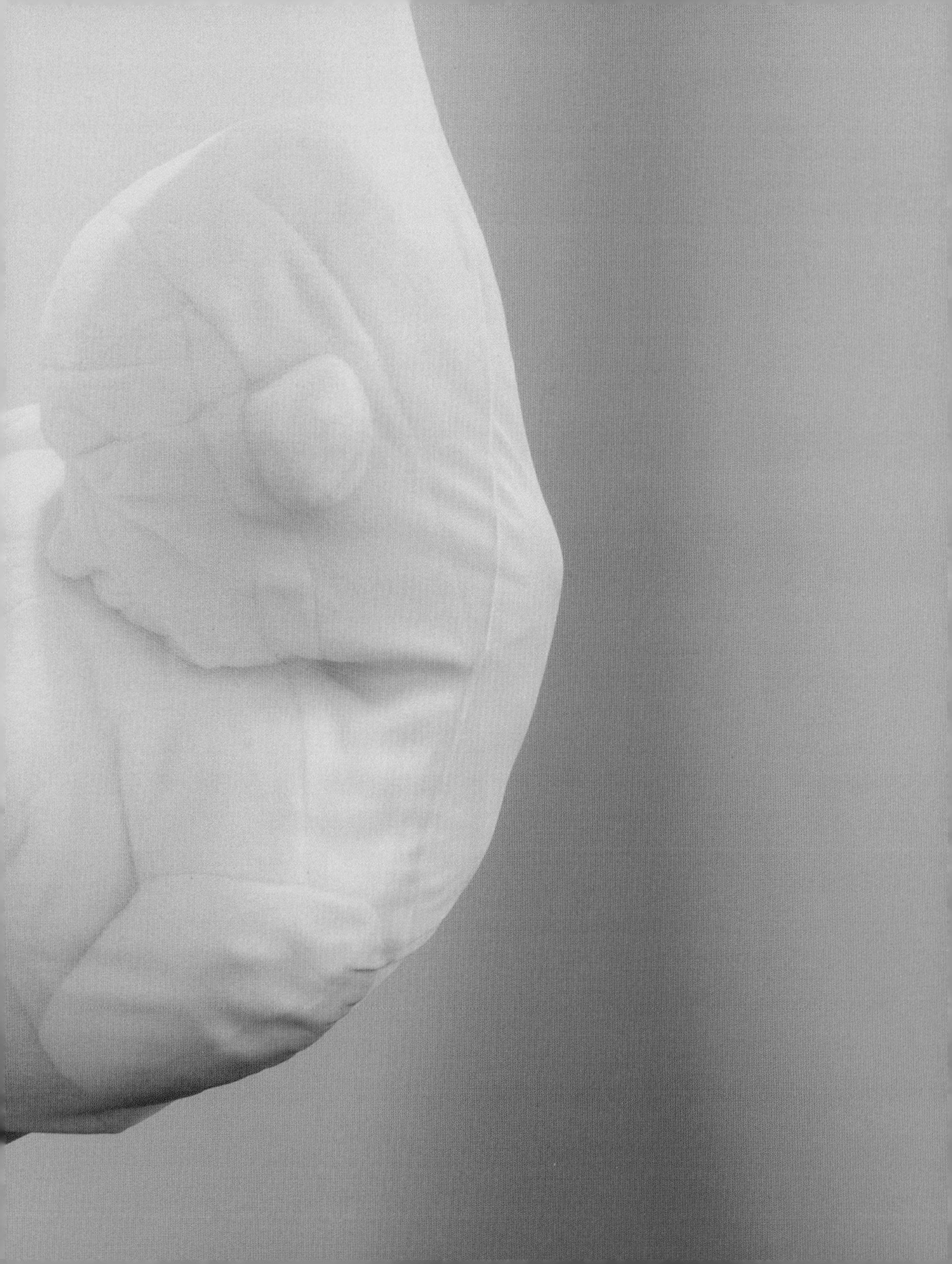

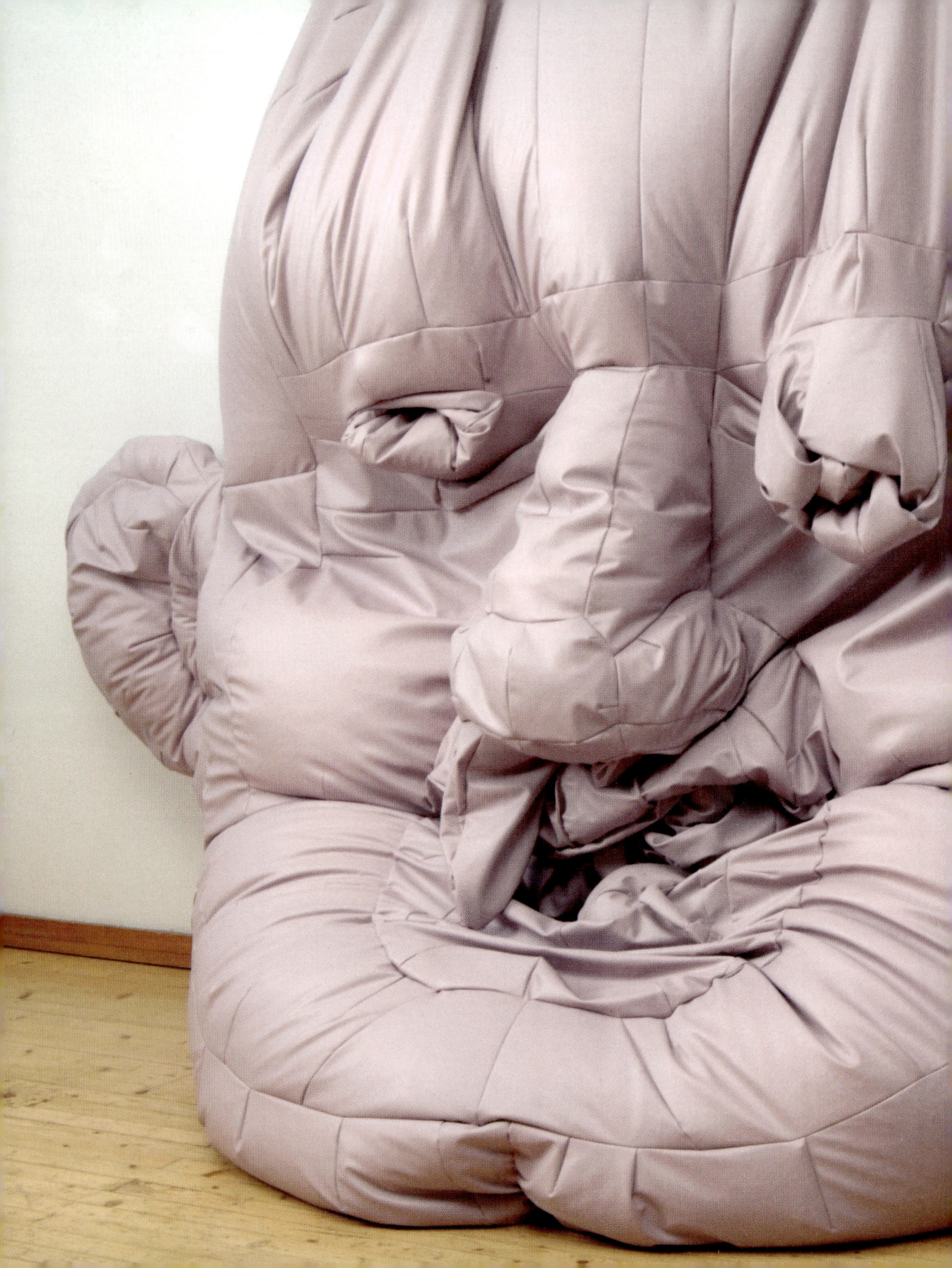

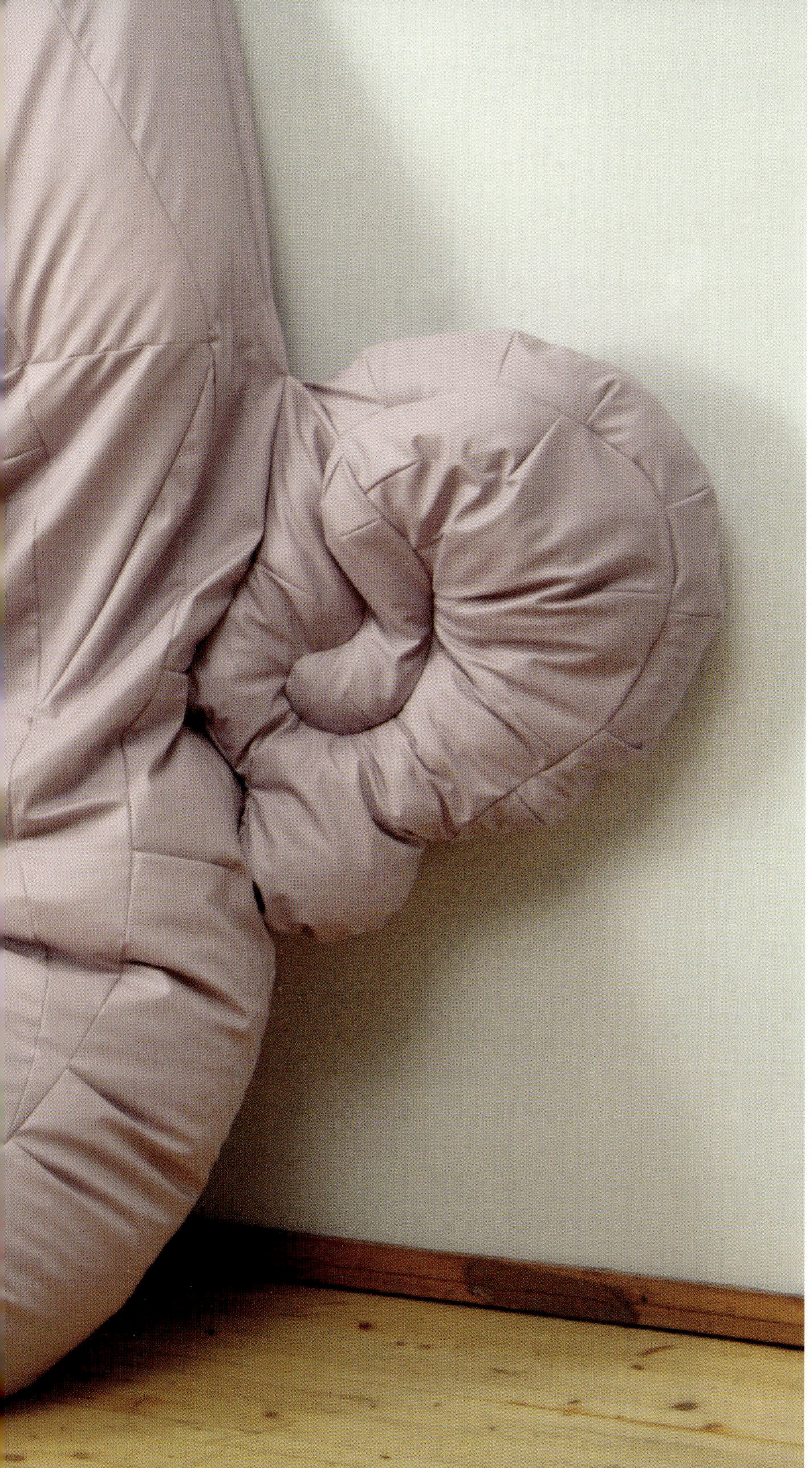

Big **Eater**
2005
Kunstleder, Füllmaterial / artificial leather, fillings
280 x 250 x 50 cm

Awake – Hibernation
2007
Kunstleder, Füllmaterial /
artificial leather, fillings
160 x 70 x 60 cm

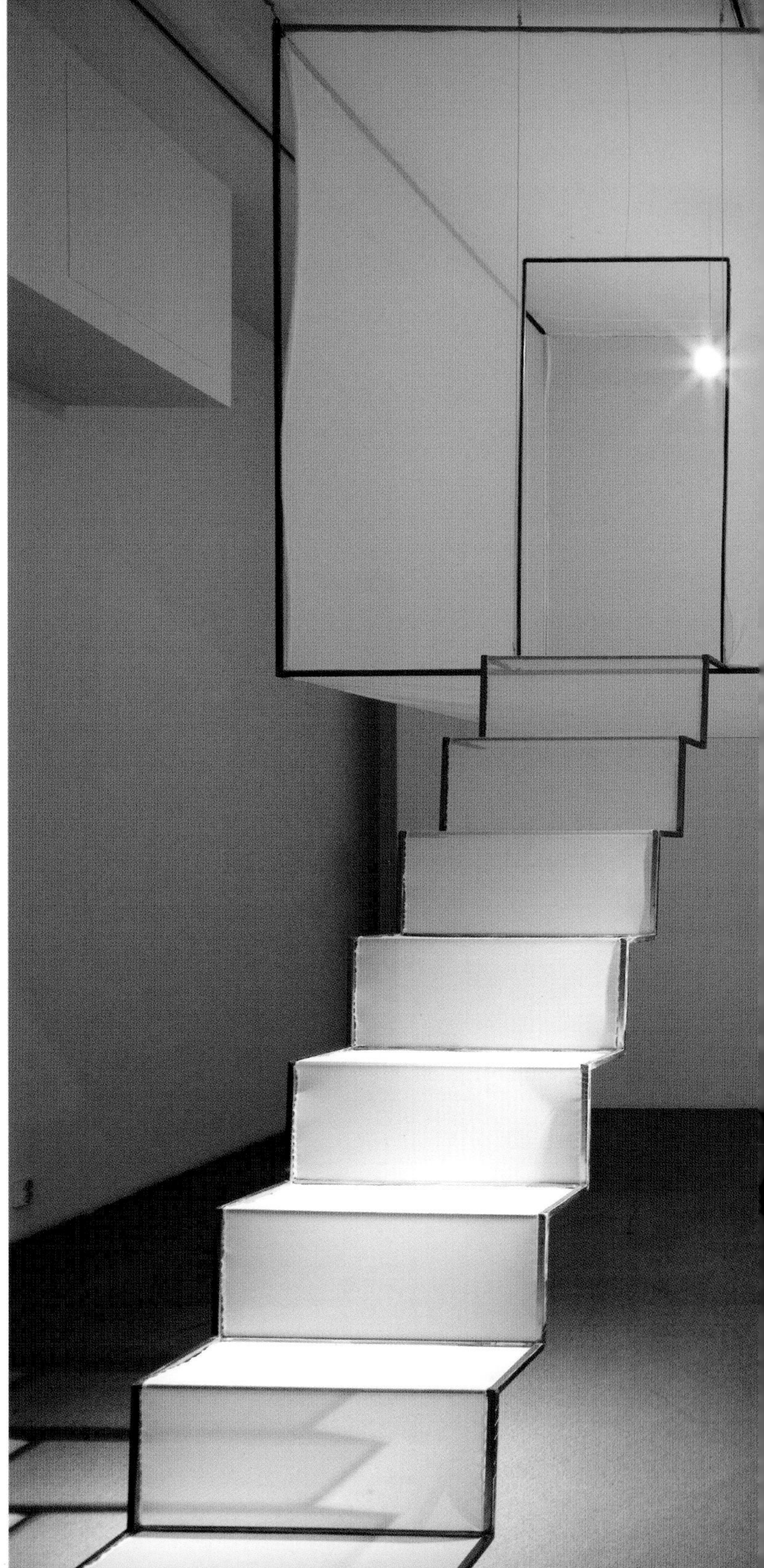

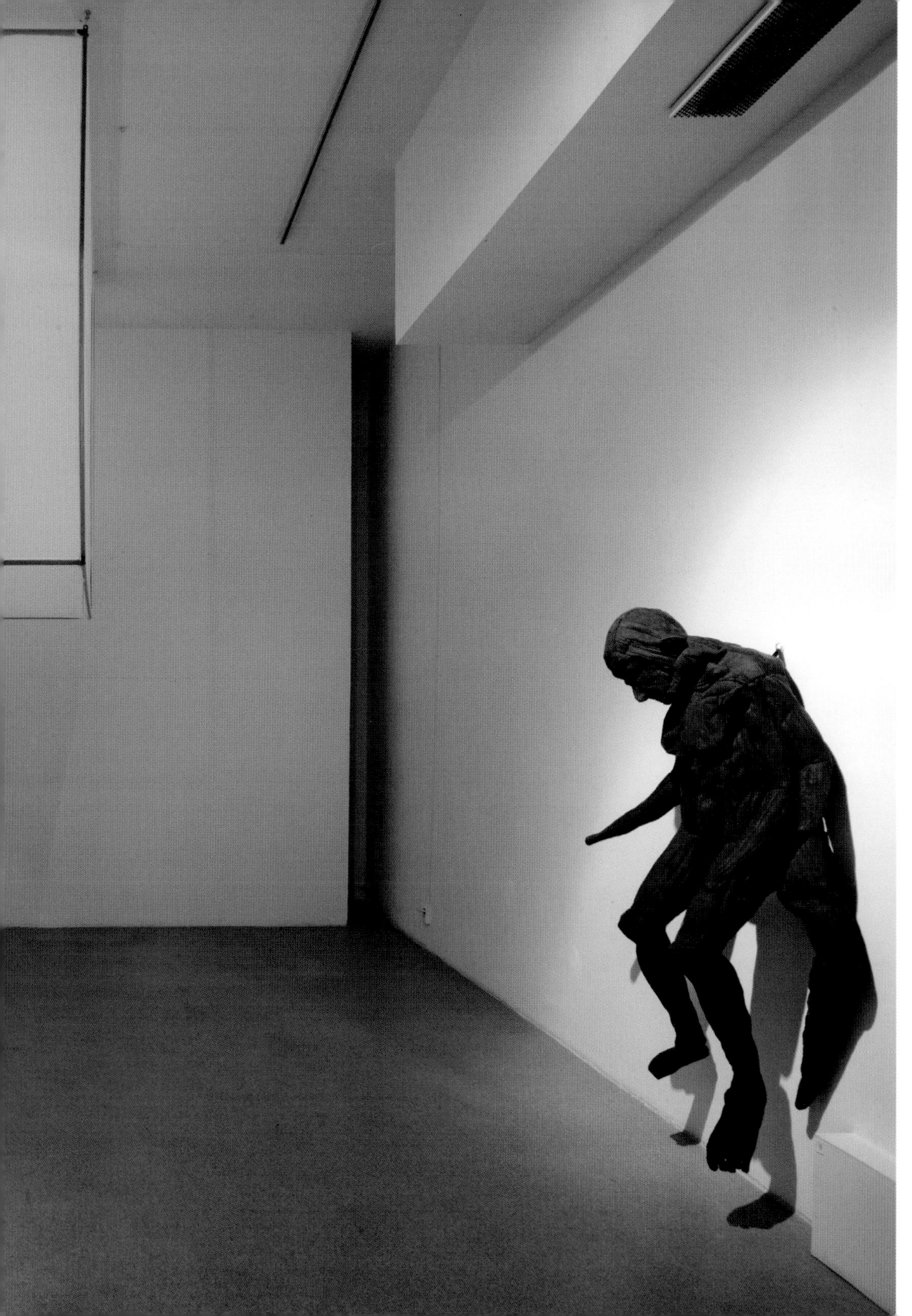

Awake – Hibernation
Detail / detail

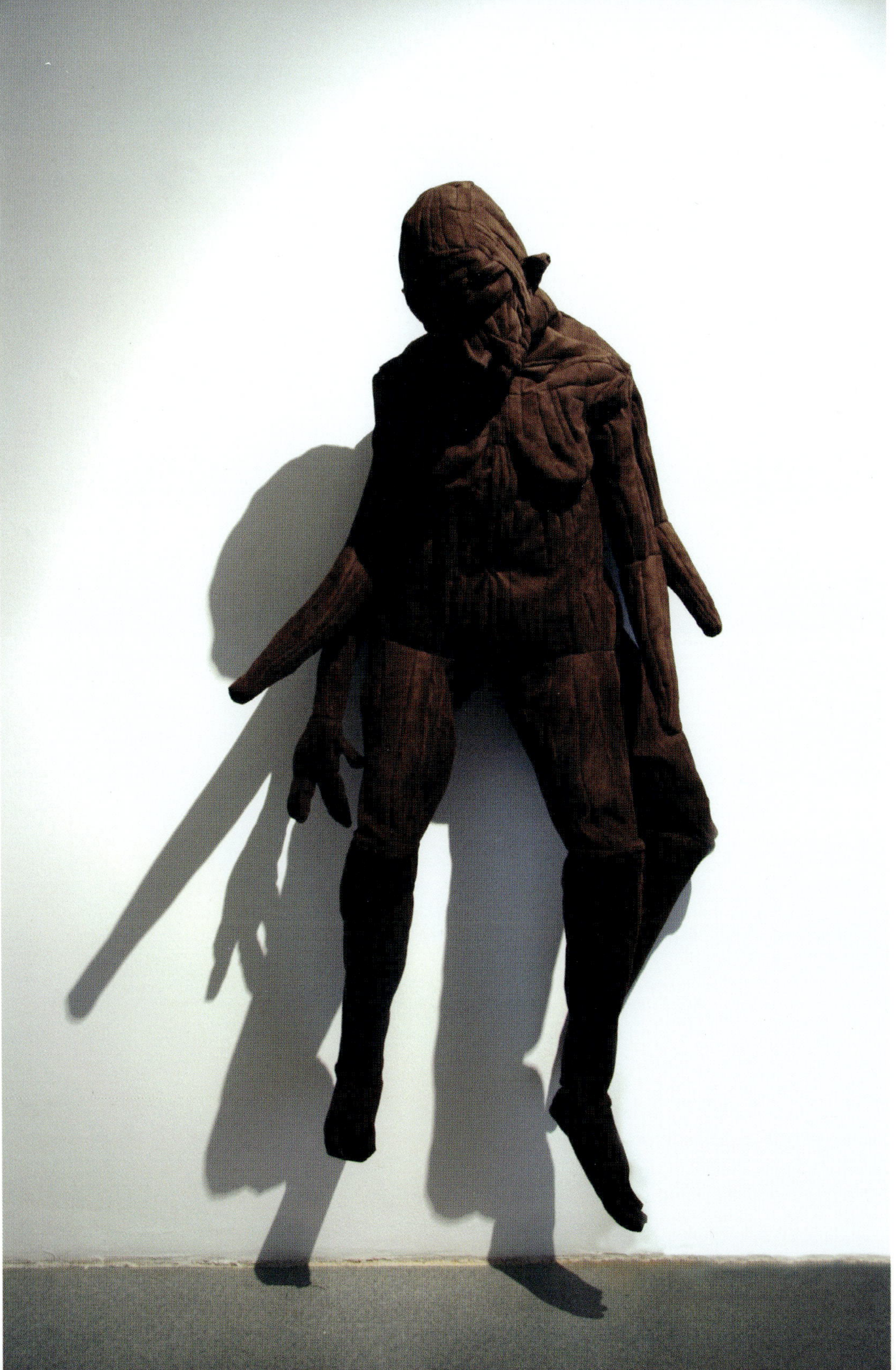

Circumstances
2004
Stoff, Stahl, Füllmaterial, Leitern /
fabric, steel, fillings, ladders
145 x 75 cm

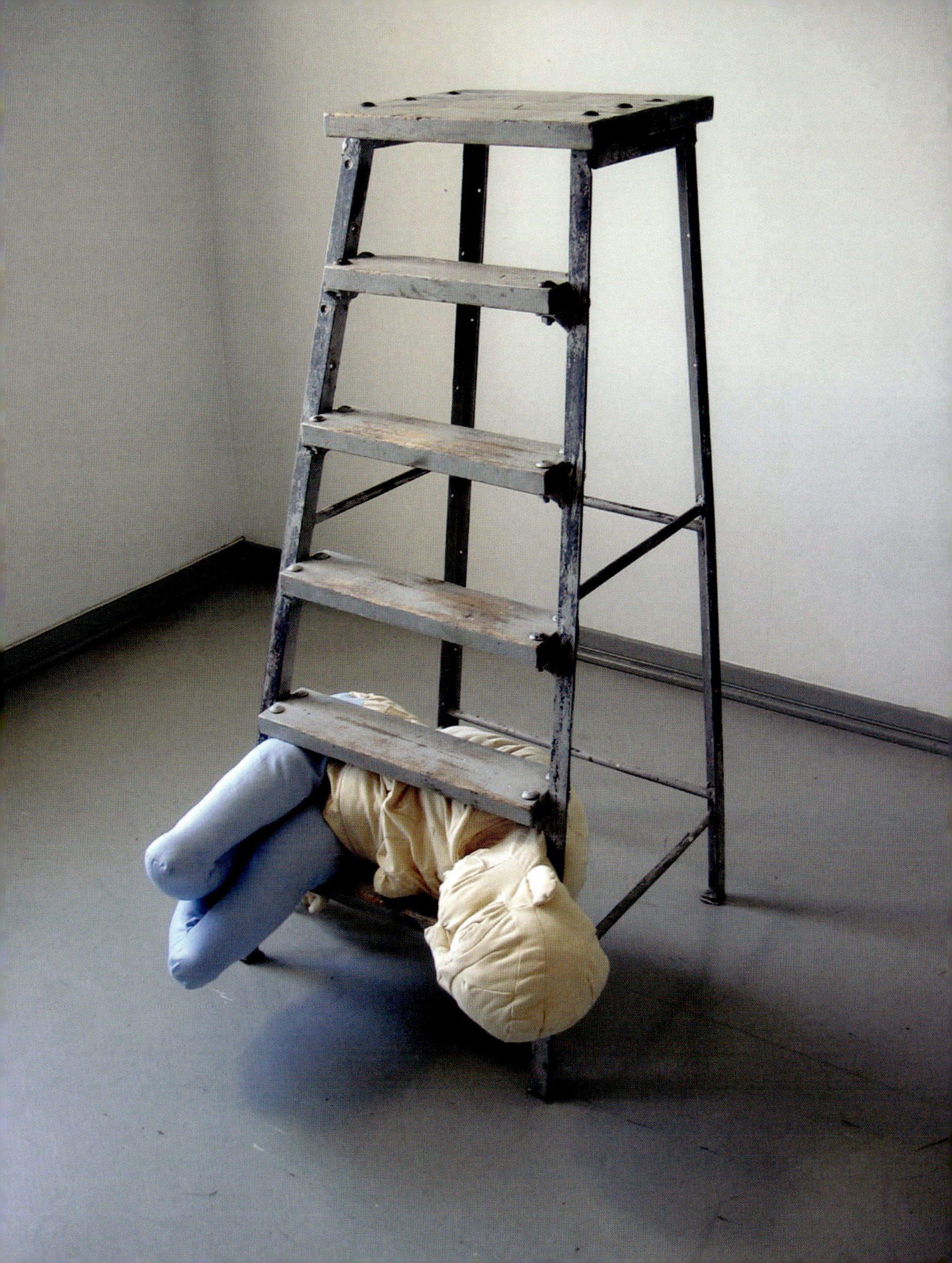

Heli Ryhänen

Lebt und arbeitet in Tampere, Finnland
Lives and works in Tampere, Finland

1971
geboren in Iisalmi, Finnland / born in Iisalmi, Finland
1990-1991
Kunstschule / Art School Liminka, Liminka
1991-1994
Kunstschule / Art School Kankaanpää, Kankaanpää
2004-2006
Akademie der Bildenden Künste, Helsinki,
Abschluss mit dem MFA / Visual Arts Academy, Helsinki, Master of Fine Arts
seit 1995 Mitglied im Künstlerverband von Tampere /
since 1995 Member of the Tampere Artist's Association
seit 1998 Mitglied im Finnischen Bildhauerverband /
since 1998 Member of The Association of Finnish Sculptors

Einzelausstellungen / Solo Exhibitions

2011
Retretti Kunstzentrum / Art Center, Punkaharju, Finnland / Finland
kunst galerie fürth, Fürth, Deutschland / Germany
2009
Galerie Husa (zusammen mit / with M. Kalkamo), Tampere, Finnland / Finland
Art and Design Gallery, UH Galleries, Hatfield, Großbritannien / Great Britain
2008
Galerie K, Huittinen, Finnland / Finland
2007
Galerie Skulptor, Helsinki, Finnland / Finland
2004
Galerie Husa, Tampere, Finnland / Finland
KU-Gallery, Kunsthalle Tallinn (zusammen mit / with A. Meskanen), Tallinn, Estland / Estonia
2002
Mältinranta Kunstzentrum, Tampere, Finnland / Finland
2001
Galerie Skulptor, Helsinki, Finnland / Finland
Galerie der Kunstschule von Kankaanpää, Finnland / Finland
2000
Galerie K, Huittinen, Finnland / Finland
Galerie Titanik, Turku, Finnland / Finland
1999
Galerie Katariina, Helsinki, Finnland / Finland
Galerie Pinacotheca, Jyväskylä, Finnland / Finland
1998
Galerie Saskia, Tampere, Finnland / Finland
Stadthalle Parkano, Parkano, Finnland / Finland

Gruppenausstellungen (Auswahl) / Group Exhibitions (Selection)

2011
Galerie 21, Malmö, Schweden / Sweden
Vestfossen Kunstlaboratorium, Vestfossen, Norwegen / Norway
2010
The Father, The Son, and The Holy Lake, Kunsthalle Helsinki, Helsinki, Finnland / Finland
Pain, Kerava Kunstmuseum, Kerava, Finnland / Finland
Talking Substance, Kunstmuseum / Art Museum Tampere, Tampere, Finnland / Finland
Demons and Darlings, Kunstmuseum / Art Museum, Oulu, Finnland / Finland
2009
Open Horizon – Treffpunkt Kunstschule Liminka, Kunstmuseum Oulu, Oulu, Finnland / Finland
Fa ej övertäska/Zeitgenössische Kunst in Finnland und Schweden,
Kunsthalle Eskilstuna, Schweden / Sweden
2008
Breaking The Mould, (1.zypriotisch-finnischer Kulturaustausch)
Panicos Maurellis Art Center, Limassol, Zypern / Cyprus
Together, Villa Roosa, Orimattila, Finnland / Finland
2007
Garden, Kunstmuseum / Art Museum Lönnström, Rauma, Finnland / Finland
Virtauksia/Streams, Kunstmuseum / Art Museum Tampere, Finnland / Finland
2006
Breaking The Mould, Stadthalle Helsinki, Helsinki, Finnland / Finland
Galerie Napa, Rovaniemi, Finnland / Finland
Shift/Scale, KUMU Kunstmuseum / Art Museum, Tallinn, Estland / Estonia
2005
Muutostiloja, SCULPTOR 2005, Finnischer Bildhauerverband / Association of Finnish Sculptors,
Amos Anderson Museum, Helsinki, Finnland / Finland
Holy/Unholy, Turku Biennal 2005, Aboa Vetus & Ars Nova, Turku, Finnland / Finland
Fuzzy Set, Kunst & Kultur, BaneGarden, Aabenraa, Dänemark / Denmark
Nord Art, KiC, Budelsdorf, Deutschland / Germany
110.Jahresausstellung Finnischer Künstler, Kunsthalle Helsinki, Finnland / Finland
2004
Art Container, Trondheim, N, & Odense, Dänemark / Denmark
2002
In and Out, Kuopio Kunstmuseum, Kuopio, Finnland / Finland
2000
1. Triennale von Pirkanmaa, Vapriikki, Tampere, Finnland / Finland
1998
Dalga, Cesme, Türkei / Turkey
1997
Phone, Städtisches Kunstmuseum / Art Museum Helsinki, Helsinki, Finnland / Finland
1996
Städtische Galerie Mitra, Lissabon, Portugal
1995
48.Jahresausstellung Junger Künstler, Kunsthalle Helsinki, Helsinki, Finnland / Finland
1994
Galerie Brinkkala, Turku, Finnland / Finland

Preise, Stipendien, Auslandsaufenthalte
Prizes, Scholarships, Residences

2009
Artist in Residence, Berlin, Deutschland / Germany (Arts Council of Satakunta)
Cité Internationale des Arts, Paris, Frankreich / France
2007
Internationales Eisenguss-Symposium, Pirkkala, Finnland / Finland
William Thuring-Preis der Finnischen Kulturstiftung
2006
Artist in Residence, Oaxaca, Mexico (gefördert vom Finnischen Künstlerverband / supported by Finnish Artist's Association)
2004
Holzbildhauer-Symposium, Lake Wrnva, Wales, Großbritannien / Great Britain
2002
Eigenart, Internationaler Papier-Workshop für Künstlerinnen, Chemnitz, Deutschland / Germany
2001
Artist in Residence, New York, USA (Visual Arts Foundation)
Sichten, Workshop für Künstlerinnen, Chemnitz, Deutschland / Germany
2000
Internationaler Eisenguss-Workshop, Veszprém, Ungarn / Hungary
1999
Artist in Residence, Oaxava, Mexico (gefördert vom Finnischen Künstlerverband / supported by Finnish Artist's Association)
1998
Internationaler Steinbildhauer-Workshop, Safaköy, Türkei / Turkey
1996
Keramik-Workshop, Lagos, Portugal

Unterstützungen u.a. von der Finnischen Kulturstiftung, dem Finnischen Staat, der Alfred Kordelin-Stiftung, der Stadt Tampere / Supported by the Finnish Cultural Foundation, the Finnish State, the Alfred Kordelin Foundation and the City of Tampere

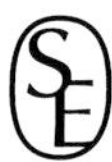

Silvana Editoriale

Projektleitung und Realisation / Produced by
Arti Grafiche Amilcare Pizzi Spa

Leitung / Direction
Dario Cimorelli

Künstlerische Leitung / Art Director
Giacomo Merli

Redaktion / Copy Editor
Ondina Granato

Layout
Anna Aurea, AM Studio

Koordination und Planung / Production Coordinator
Michela Bramati

Redaktionsassistenz / Editorial Assistant
Emma Altomare

Bildredaktion / Iconographic Office
Deborah D'Ippolito

Presse- und Öffentlichkeitsarbeit / Press Office
Lidia Masolini, press@silvanaeditoriale.it

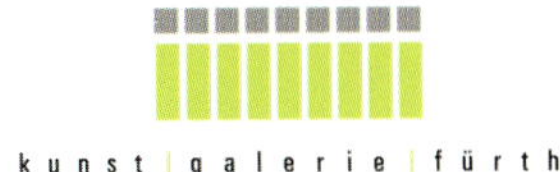

Text
Hans-Peter Miksch

Übersetzungen / Translations
Dr. Gerrit Jackson, Berlin; Sato Leinonen, Tampere

Fotos / Photos
Pekka Helin, Ilari Järvinen, Patrik Rastenberger, Heli Ryhänen, Jussi Tiainen

Diese Publikation erscheint anlässlich der Ausstellung von Heli Ryhänen
in der kunst galerie fürth, Fürth, Deutschland, vom 18.März bis zum 1.Mai 2011.
www.kunst-galerie-fuerth.de
Dank an FRAME, Finnish Fund for Art Exchange, HypoKulturstiftung, München,
Firma Schredl, Fürth, Freundeskreis der kunst galerie fürth.

This catalogue is published on the occasion of the exhibition of Heli Ryhänen
in the Art Gallery fürth, Fürth, Germany, 18 March - 1 May 2011.
www.kunst-galerie-fuerth.de
Thanks to FRAME, Finnish Fund for Art Exchange, HypoKulturstiftung, Munchen,
Schredl, Fürth, Freundeskreis der kunst galerie fürth.

Sponsors

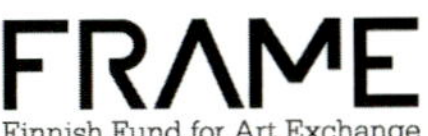

HYPO-KULTURSTIFTUNG

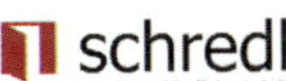

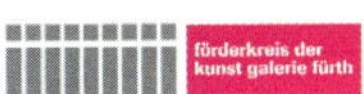

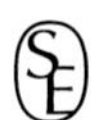

Silvana Editoriale Spa

via Margherita De Vizzi, 86
20092 Cinisello Balsamo, Milano
tel. 02 61 83 63 37
fax 02 61 72 464
www.silvanaeditoriale.it

Reproduktionen, Druck und Bindung von
Arti Grafiche Amilcare Pizzi Spa
Cinisello Balsamo, Mailand
Reproductions, printing and binding by
Arti Grafiche Amilcare Pizzi Spa
Cinisello Balsamo, Milan

Gedruckt im März 2011
Printed March 2011